D0986603

AN OUTLIER'S TRIBE

To Susan,   08/26/21

Thank you for your support!

— *[signature]*

AN OUTLIER'S TRIBE

MORGAN K. EDWARDS

NEW DEGREE PRESS

COPYRIGHT © 2020 MORGAN K. EDWARDS

All rights reserved.

AN OUTLIER'S TRIBE

ISBN   978-1-64137-965-6   *Paperback*

          978-1-64137-792-8   *Kindle Ebook*

          978-1-64137-793-5   *Ebook*

This book is dedicated to my dad, who passed away during my senior year of high school in 2017 following a battle with ALS.

Dad,

You fought with incredible strength and somehow always managed to have a gentle smile and an appreciation for life, even when the world was crumbling around [and within] you.

To the most sage and supportive person I have ever known: thanks for showing me how to be my own outlier and teaching me everything I know. This one's for you.

Love you, Doc

CONTENTS

Respect the elders.
Embrace the new.
Encourage the impractical and
improbable, without bias.

—VIN SCELSA'S THREE
ESSENTIAL COMMANDMENTS

Have fun.
Try your best.
I'm proud of you. But more importantly,
you should be proud of yourself.

—DAD A.K.A. THE DOC A.K.A. DOCTOR J

FOREWORD

———

When I got off the bus in Northern Ireland and bounded up the mildew-stained stairs of my brother's sublet, eagerly asking him about what he'd been up to in the months since we'd last seen each other, I never expected him to casually throw "thinking about writing a book" into the long list of endeavors he'd been pursuing. At the same time, I wasn't the least bit surprised.

When people ask me about my relationship with Morgan, it is easy to sum up: we're close. I'm the [self-proclaimed] "favorite child," but he's always been the child deserving of this title. Upon his arrival into this world, I, at age four, threw a Category V tantrum. I'm talking no-shoes, lots-of-tears, drag-me-by-one-snotty-arm kind of tantrum. When my grandparents were finally able to coax me into the Morgantown, West Virginia, hospital room where my brother had just been born, I fixated my eyes on the TV and refused to acknowledge his shiny new existence whatsoever. He was not the younger sister for whom I had put in a special request and not so subtly demanded my mother give birth to—you know, the kind from whom you can steal clothes and talk with about crushes. Throughout his infancy, I loved to convince him he was adopted or a mistake (or both), much to our parents' chagrin. In my defense, all I can say is, heavy is the head that wears the crown of Oldest Sibling.

Ironically, my little brother ended up being not just a confidant (with a closet I oft frequented) but also the person I look up to most in this world. For the twenty years I have known him, he has served as a constant source of entertainment, empathy, and eager energy—always ready to make you laugh, hold you tight, and ask you a billion questions about whatever obscure thing he happens to want to mull over at the moment. He wants to know anything and everything, and once he knows it, it sticks around in that big brain of his and never leaves (for better or for worse). He's a literal human sponge, and you have to be careful because he will squeeze out your own words, in addition to the words of several other relevant quotes and facts he's memorized, and use them against you when you least expect it. Morgan will always hear you out, and then he will respond with the wit and wisdom of a one-hundred-year-old Buddhist monk. The questions I inevitably end up asking him on a daily basis are, 1) "How do you know this?" and, more importantly, 2) "Why do you know this?" His answer? "I don't know, because, I just do."

When people ask about where we're from, it is far less easy to sum up, as you'll see from Morgan's devotion of an entire book to that very end. I've spent entire hours of my college political science classes trying to describe the place and people that are Appalachia—trying to make my fellow students and professors understand the existence and significance of this place I myself haven't figured out, despite the nearly two decades I spent growing up there.

After one particular political science class, my professor approached me, a book in her hands. "Here," she said, extending it out to me. "Everything that comes out of your mouth sounds like this book—you've got to read it. Here's my copy. I'd love to hear your thoughts when you've finished." It was J. D. Vance's *Hillbilly Elegy*. I flew through that book, reading it cover to cover in a matter of days, prying it open when I should have been prepping for another essay or listening to another class's lecture. By our class the following week, I had written an entire page of notes and arrived with the book in hand, far more prepared to discuss domestic policy in impoverished regions like mine than that day's assigned reading.

I loved *Hillbilly Elegy* because it was the first book I had ever read that even made mention of my neck of the woods. I was able to anticipate the endings to most of Vance's sentences, finishing them in my head before reading the words. I devoured every descriptive detail of each page, sometimes re-reading the sentences so many times I wasn't sure I hadn't written them myself. For all the criticism and controversy I have since heard in response to *Hillbilly Elegy*, the memoir remains one of the only texts in which I have been fully engrossed in the nitty-gritty details, details in which I have been able to see myself.

Several professors throughout my college career, with whom I intentionally or unintentionally shared snippets of home, urged me to write about the experience of my hometown. "It's so unique," they'd say. "It's not very often you hear about a Middlebury student from this type of background! People would find it very interesting."

But I could never bring myself to do it. I had spent every waking (and sleeping) minute of my high school career working toward a way to leave, eventually happily ending up some 560 miles and nine hours away at a small liberal arts college in Vermont. When college peers spoke of homesickness as they adjusted to life away from home, I realized it was a feeling I had never experienced. I didn't understand what it meant to long for where you come from; I only knew what it felt like to run hard and fast away from it, without looking back.

I carried a lot of bitterness toward Appalachia throughout college and, if we're being completely honest, I still do. It's a place that often turned its back on me and anyone else who questioned it. I spent a lot of time feeling suffocated, misunderstood, and fed up, to a degree that surpassed normal teen angst. The only identity I formed in my adolescence seemed to be one in pure opposition to the region that raised me. That bitterness was only compounded when I arrived at college and learned of all the opportunities and ways of thinking I had missed out on because of my childhood in Appalachia. My mom always said if I didn't have anything nice to say, I shouldn't say anything at all, and I never felt that sentiment stronger than while trying to make sense of home. After spending so much time and effort distancing myself from it, I had little desire to relive it in any way.

That is, until Morgan wrote this book.

Take the feeling I had toward *Hillbilly Elegy* and multiply it ten-fold, and that's what I felt the first time I read a draft chapter from *An Outlier's Tribe*. Like Vance's book, Morgan's provides rich imagery of a misunderstood area, which he bolsters with region-specific statistics and nuances with a variety of lived experiences. He elucidates a landscape with the personal and the political, shedding light on true experiences that I've previously only been able to offer glimpses of. Written from the unique vantage point of a young person still very much balancing the dichotomous worlds of Appalachia and New England, *An Outlier's Tribe* gives Appalachia's residents the deserving benefit of the doubt that I have found difficult to do in my own interactions. Above all, this book acknowledges that there are still questions left unanswered and demonstrates why the rest of the country should give a damn and delve into those questions. It shows us why Appalachia is not a forgotten tale of the distant past but rather a complex, current way of life that could not be more relevant to today's social, political, and economic backdrop.

If you're like me, as you read, you might find yourself formulating a reactionary response, comeback, or question to a certain passage. Instead, I urge you to just keep reading, because I promise you that the very thing you're wondering about is the very point Morgan gets to next. I encourage you to drop your preconceived notions at the door and instead listen with an open mind. It will allow you to take away something big from this book.

I so admire the depth, perspective, and understanding my brother has brought to *An Outlier's Tribe*. It is far more patient, understanding, and vulnerable than I ever could have managed. In fact, I'm afraid this foreword will not do it the justice it deserves. Reading Morgan's words has helped me let go of much of my resentment and instead replaced it with a more profound layer of comprehension and compassion. It has allowed me to bore through my layers of bias to the slab of gratitude I keep for all the opportunities, experiences, and thoughts I have as a result of growing up in this place.

Appalachia has given me perspective, and Morgan's book has reminded me of this perspective. It takes a village, and though Appalachia is not the "village" I would have chosen for myself or my brother to be raised in, I wouldn't change it if I could. *An Outlier's Tribe* affirms that although I often feel my identity exists in opposition to the place, Appalachia is as integral to the landscape of American identity as it is to who I have become. And after all, Appalachia raised my brother, and he's the best person I know, so it must be doing something right.

—Georgia Grace Edwards

PREFACE

———

It's not often you wake up to a LinkedIn message from a Georgetown professor asking if you'd like to write a book (Thanks, Eric Koester). *Hmm, sounds intriguing and random and also probably like spam.* Even less frequently do you open said message anyway—which appears at first glance to be another mass-generated message cluttering the ole inbox (Sorry, Eric Koester)—and think *A book? Yeah, why the hell not!*

After looking into it and confirming it was, in fact, a legit book writing program—at least as best I could tell via the Internet and a brief Skype convo with Eric—I decided to just see where it would lead until I was bound by having to make an official decision. In the meantime, I put it on the back burner. I was in Northern Ireland for the summer, making a concerted effort to be present and soak it up as best I could. Besides, between the academic, athletic, and extracurricular (and oh, yeah, social life) demands of the soon-to-begin fall semester—coupled with the litany of other prospective projects and activities on my mind—I just did not know if a book was feasible. And I still wasn't 100 percent positive it wasn't a scam.

But it simply kept nagging at me. I would be savoring a Guinness in a remote Irish village or hauling ass up a sixth-century Atlantic island monastery—totally living in the moment—and all of a sudden, I would drift back to the book. That goddamn book. Maybe I should go for it after all. I'd love to write about how it was meant to be, how it had always been my dream, yada yada yada. Truthfully, however, I was drawn to the idea because I thought it sounded totally wacky. I mean, when else in my life was I going to do this? Perhaps I had always envisioned writing *something, somewhere, someday*, but, of course, that was not guaranteed. I realized I would always be busy, and there would never truly be a good time to commit to such an undertaking, so the time was now. As I pieced together what I wanted to write about, I realized it could be a nice capstone of the first twenty years of my life. I could use the book as a way to meaningfully consider my upbringing and the place that shaped me.

I'm glad that I decided to reply to that fateful LinkedIn message and jump in headfirst. For the past year, amidst the chaotic world of college, grieving my dad, a pandemic, and a personal drawn-out tussle with pneumonia this spring, the book has been a constant in my life. It has served as a guiding goal to which I have been able to orient myself.

There were also many times when, quite frankly, it was the last thing I wanted to be doing. It felt like an omnipresent cloud hanging over me, nagging me when I least sought it. There is nothing worse than slogging through some dense assigned journal article or grinding out a class research paper and letting out a sigh of relief, only to immediately be struck with: *Shit, now it's on to the book.* I often felt like I missed out on other things peers were doing as I plugged away in solitude. But, as my mom (correctly) reminded me countless times when I felt that way, this was a challenge I had brought upon myself—a journey that has been one of the most difficult and rewarding undertakings of my life.

For the past year, the book has constantly consumed my thoughts and precipitated far too many nights where I have lain awake unable to turn my brain off, making hurried trips to scribble an idea into my notepad at two a.m. It has just as often brought about the contrasting bouts of writer's block where my mind has felt empty as I restlessly paced in front of my desk. It has provoked doubts, cultivated grit, pushed me to embrace vulnerability, and even given rise to some unironically hilarious to-do lists. See if you can spot the odd one out: "Do laundry, pick up mail, write a book."

There's a beauty in the journey I have learned to embrace. And, in a way, it has even come full circle. I wrote much of the book at school and unexpectedly completed it at home after returning due to COVID-19. Physically straddling the divergent environments of which I speak in the book has infused the writing process with bits of each, thus bringing in new points of view and enriching the journey as a whole.

I am proud to have persisted on the journey, although as I posited to my mom during a particular moment of frustration: *I'm pulling a Trump and using a ghostwriter next time.* I stand by that statement.

INTRODUCTION

Nov. 9, 2016: As I drive overlooking the rolling Appalachian Mountains dotted with strip mines, I can only imagine what will transpire today in my high school. I try to mentally brace myself for the inevitable, though there's a weird part of me that is genuinely curious to see how my fellow classmates will react to last night's news.

Passing through the halls on my way to class, I can't help but marvel at the sheer absurdity of it all. Copious amounts of Confederate flag attire, the echo of "Trump Train" chants ricocheting off lockers, the flashes of red MAGA hats in the hallways, the *click* of steel-toed Carolina boots on the stairs. Granted, this is nothing new in my deeply conservative town, nestled in the impoverished hills and hollers of Western Maryland. However, this is on a new level—people aren't just happy, they're emboldened. Trump's surprise late-night victory has injected new life into an otherwise monotonous school day. It seems even some of my normally apathetic peers, the "too cool for school" bunch, are fully engaged—at least politically speaking. Trump has given them something to care about, to be proud of, to flaunt.

For some, this show of support is in good faith; that is, it's born out of a genuine joy in Trump's win. For others, it's all about instigation. Triggering the snowflake libs is fun, right? What better way to provoke the few existing liberals than by openly chanting "MAGA" at the top of your lungs and ribbing them with a, "So, how about that election last night?" comment.

No matter the motivation, the result is clear: my peers are visibly empowered by Trump's presidential win. Empowered to don sweatshirts toting the Stars and Bars in a state that never even seceded from the Union. Empowered to proudly advocate for a man who has spent his entire life in private jets, penthouse high-rises, and lavish golf resorts—as far removed as ever from the Appalachian legacies of black lung—and who ostensibly thinks "clean coal" means physically scrubbing it.

Amidst this crowd—which I find myself likening more to a rally at Mar-a-Lago than a high school trigonometry class—stands me. And by standing, I mean standing out. My family's values, behaviors, and tendencies could not stray further from the prevailing culture.

You see, in my rural area, small-town politics pervades seemingly every aspect of life. One's family origins and "who you know" are often determining factors for sports, awards, local government, etc. It's big news if you "stray too far" and don't stick around the area. Not only are both my parents from the Northeast, but they also are not your prototypical Appalachians in any sense of the word. My dad, especially, was always an outlier. He embraced his quirkiness, sporting a ponytail, being a Grateful Dead aficionado, naming our dog after the founder of Afrobeat (Fela Kuti), and unabashedly wearing Jerry Garcia ties to work every day as a college psychology professor. He was prudent and sagacious, constantly reiterating profound ideas of embracing the new, believing in karma, being zen, valuing experiences over possessions, and living in the moment. One can only imagine how his "transcendentalist-esque" personality and idiosyncrasies meshed with the conservative social fabric of Appalachia.

As for my mom, she is a former social worker who later became involved in local politics as a city council member. For the majority of her tenure, her council colleagues consisted primarily of white men over sixty who were born and raised in the area and held deeply conservative views. Contrast that with a pink "pussyhat"-wearing, Women's March-participating, Carole King-loving woman in my mom. I like to think of her as the Alexandria Ocasio-Cortez of Appalachia.

Then there's my sister. A fiercely independent and open-minded free spirit, she relentlessly chases new experiences. Her life motto? "What have I never done before? What am I least likely to ever do again? Well, that's what I'm going to do." She is driven by the ideal of exposing herself to new and unpredictable situations, places, and experiences as a means to broaden her horizons, become a more informed and empathetic individual, and better understand the world around her. This is the guiding philosophy that has brought her to twenty-four countries by the age of twenty-four, earn a Fulbright in the Czech Republic, study abroad at Fidel Castro's alma mater in Havana, appear in an Ethiopian beer commercial, work as a glacier guide on the Mendenhall Glacier in Alaska, and most recently, found a startup called SheFly centered around making outdoor pants that allow women to quite literally answer nature's call—in other words, feminist pee pants.

At this point, I'm sure it comes as no surprise that I likewise do not reflect the environment in which I grew up. I'm a political junkie involved in progressive politics with experience working on campaigns (shout-out Beto O'Rourke!), participating in senate programs, doing impressions (Bernie Sanders being my specialty), and even founding and co-hosting a political podcast on Apple. I have a bucket list of places to travel, complete with hundreds of countries and tens of thousands of locations—a list I started researching and compiling at age ten. I enjoy mindfulness and meditation, Stephen Colbert, and discussions about Medicare for All. These aren't exactly the types of hobbies and interests that jibe well in an area of coal mines, camouflage, and Confederates.

***

Back at school, looking around, I feel totally isolated, disconnected from my peers, unable to understand those around me and the region in which I live, and confused at what seems to be patently obvious cognitive dissonance at play. *How could everybody here so blatantly vote against their own interests?* I wonder. *How is Donald Trump our president? Donald Trump? DONALD TRUMP?* Today is the day my long-held feelings clearly manifest themselves at the surface: I do not feel at home in my hometown.

***

As a nation, we have become increasingly tribal in recent years. Political polarization and partisan animosity are higher than at any point in the last quarter-century.[1] We get our news from different sources, existing in personally-curated digital echo chambers. We feel visceral disdain for the other side, and we rejoice when they suffer a setback. We even physically cluster ourselves into self-selected homogeneous communities—a process journalist Bill Bishop calls "the big sort."[2]

But what about those who do not fit into these neatly separated parts of America? The heartland is not a monolith after all. Neither are the liberal coasts. Growing up in Appalachia, I often felt out of place—an outlier whose background, worldview, core beliefs, and values fundamentally clashed with the norm. I found myself amongst the opposite tribe, a rogue blue dot in a sea of red.

I now find myself calling Maine home while studying at Bowdoin College. Here on the pine-studded Atlantic coast, my peers enthusiastically discuss democratic socialism, reflect upon their gap years, and don Patagonia pullovers. Navigating the striking juxtaposition that is the dichotomy between my upbringing and my current home-away-from-home has taught me more about the world than time spent in any classroom.

Even amongst many of my sharp, worldly Bowdoin peers, Appalachia is an enigma. Few know what it is, let alone what it's all about. When asked details about home, I often struggle to have the right answer, having felt like an outsider in the region myself. How do I convey my messy, conflicting, and not always fully-formed feelings? Moreover, how do I

---

1   "Partisanship and Political Animosity in 2016," *Pew Research Center*, June 22, 2016.

2   Bill Bishop, *The Big Sort: Why the Clustering of Like-Minded America Is Tearing Us Apart*, (Boston: Houghton Mifflin, 2008).

condense Appalachia—with all its nuance, contradiction, and perplexity—and the profound effect it has had on my upbringing into a soundbite or a lunch conversation? Wrestling with such considerations encouraged me to begin thinking about reconciling with my past in a more formal and comprehensive fashion.

I wanted to write this book because the further I am physically and temporally removed from the region in which I grew up, the more I anticipate feeling disconnected—unable to meaningfully grapple with that era of my life. Further, in currently attending a school that represents the antithesis of home, I look back from a unique vantage point on the first twenty years of my life.

I aim to grapple with my experiences growing up in Appalachia, come to better understand a place where I mostly felt out of place, and explore how I've existed in two vastly different environments. While it was incredibly frustrating to grow up in a region so opposite to my core worldview, I feel very grateful to have done so. It has given me a perspective on an oft-misunderstood and forgotten part of the country. It has shaped me in innumerable ways—some of which I am only now starting to uncover. For all its drawbacks, being an outlier had unintended benefits.

The act itself of writing this book is pushing me to confront my past, reflect on my experiences, and parse through the ambiguity of both. I don't have all the answers, and I don't claim to. These are just the thoughts, opinions, and experiences of one person. It represents a snapshot of how I felt then and how I feel as I write. I recognize things may change and I may feel differently as time passes; yet, I hope in the process of my personal introspection I have provided something of value to you, my reader, perhaps by spurring you to self-reflect, critically think about your upbringing, or better understand the polarized state of our country. Whether you have felt like an outsider in any way (politically, socially, culturally, etc.), are concerned about the increasing division in this country, or are simply interested in learning more about Appalachia and the nurture side of nature/nurture, *An Outlier's Tribe* will introduce you to my stories of trying to find my tribe in a time of tribalism.

PART 1:

THE PLACE

CHAPTER 1 –

HOME

___

When asked where I'm from, I respond, "Maryland." Then I immediately move to modify my answer. "Well, Western Maryland... about as far west as you can go, right in the little panhandle that juts out into West Virginia... about two-and-a-half hours west of DC... it's basically West Virginia... you know what, West Virginia. I'm from West Virginia."

It's easiest just to simplify and claim a different statehood. After all, Western Maryland shares little in common with our counterparts "downstate" in the Baltimore/DC metropolitan area—a fact of which its residents have taken to heart, perhaps too much so. When I was growing up, some area residents became involved with a secessionist movement calling for Western Maryland to separate from the rest of the state. I remember high school teachers prominently displaying "Liberate Western Maryland" stickers on their classroom doors, town hall meetings to discuss exit strategy, and Facebook being overrun by a group that accumulated close to 10,000 likes.

The group decried the socialist "despots" in Annapolis who supported a welfare state, higher taxes, gun control, abortion, and any number of other totalitarian measures, all the while ignoring the rural Western counties. They likened the movement to an "abused spouse... who must stay and continue to be abused," tied themselves to Brexit and other historical independence movements in the former USSR, and unironically co-opted self-determination rhetoric more reminiscent of Che Guevara than a hillbilly manifesto. For your viewing pleasure and convenience, what follows is a handpicked list of comments that littered my Facebook feed:

"There is a West Virginia... What's stopping a West Maryland?"
"All you need is the will and desire to do so."
"End of Tyranny of King O'Malley!"
"The Time Has Come for 51!"
"The [state] motto should be 'We're the smart ones.'"
"The rallying cry among the colonists was 'Join or Die.'
We now need a new one for our initiative and I suggest
'Separate and Live.'"[3]

Man, I never thought I'd long for the days when Facebook was a haven for sharing stupid cat videos, poking people, and posting status updates about what you had for breakfast.

I'm sorry—you're quite simply not freedom fighters freeing yourselves from the repressive reach of Soviet Russia or revolutionaries decolonizing from an imperial regime (albeit the socialist language is a nice touch for a movement protesting so-called "socialism"). You're disgruntled by the tyranny that is a public healthcare exchange and a gas tax that ironically funds state highway snow removal in our

---

3   "Western Maryland: A New State Initiative (@FreeWesternMaryland)," Facebook page, *Facebook*.

own disproportionately mountainous part of the state. Not to mention the injustice of hunting limits on the number of bears that can be killed.[4] This is a rural county that feels under-represented (for which I do think a legitimate case can be made) and differs politically from the state as a whole. It is not a paragon of oppression warranting independence. My personal favorite has to be "Just curious would [it] be feasible to hook up with either West Virginia or Pennsylvania?"—as if this harebrained attempt to upend US state sovereignty is not only realistic but merely a simple, laid-back endeavor (Just phone up West Virginia and see if they'll take us in!).

I can't forget the others who asked seemingly fundamental, yet neglected questions ("What will the name be?"), a matter that appeared to be overlooked by many consumed with secessionist zeal. The answer, according to one user: "Liberty."

***

Liberty. So, I guess that's where I'm from. Perhaps that should be my response. Short, succinct, evoking of a patriotic ideal— seems like a better alternative to my rambling attempt to modify "Maryland."

I do concede that the dichotomy between Western Maryland and the rest of the state is striking. Of course I am not a fan of secession (don't take it from me, take it from the Maryland political scientist who called it "one of the stupidest political ideas of the twenty-first century"), but I recognize that politically, socially, culturally, topographically, and in

---

4   Dan Rodricks, "Hefty price tag for Western Maryland succession," *The Baltimore Sun*, September 14, 2013.

just about every other aspect, there exists more than one "Maryland."[5]

There's even this landmark called Sideling Hill about forty miles east of my town that seemingly acts as a physical gateway to the West. It's a deep man-made notch excavated from the top of a ridge to allow the highway—which connects one end of the state to the other—to pass through. As you drive through the exposed rock lining the mountain pass, it's as if you are physically straddling the division between Appalachia and the rest of the state. Only two and a half hours removed by car, my area feels worlds away from DC, Baltimore, Annapolis, and civilization in general; their liberal politics, affluence, and stateliness a far cry from the abandoned coal mines and four-wheeler tracks crisscrossing my county.

Home to roughly 9,000, my town of Frostburg sits perched 2,000 feet up in the mountains. Driving in, you're immediately welcomed by Sheetz (Mid-Atlantic gas station, convenience store, and popular local hot spot), a car dealership with a huge roadside "TRUMP" sign, the high school, and the churches— that is, if you happen to be Christian (Protestant preferred). That's right, the dilapidated *Frostburg Churches Welcome You* sign prominently displays emblems of 18 churches (representing seemingly every Protestant denomination) for a town of 9,000! Run some quick mental math and you've got yourself a church for every 500 (Christian) folks.

Town has one main drag, which owes its vibrance in large part to the local university. We are fortunate to have it in our community, and it is much of the reason my town has fared better than other local municipalities. Small businesses line Main Street, many of them catering to the college students

---

5   Herbert Smith, qtd. in Ibid.

that boost our town population to 150 percent of summertime levels. We somehow have a staggering seven pizza joints, albeit not quite enough to top the Protestant church-to-person ratio. The big events on Friday nights are high school football games or the rendezvous in which some of my peers would park their F-150s in a circle in the designated parking lot of choice that particular night to hang out, inspect each other's trucks, and chew dip.

Head south and you'll pass coal mines, Republican clubs, and American Legions on your way "down the crick" as you trace the meandering Georges Creek before it flows into the Potomac. One's pronunciation of "creek" is a surefire way to root out the real locals from the outsiders. Think of it like the Appalachian equivalent of "pahk the cah in Hahvahd Yahhhd." When declining population levels forced the high schools "down the crick" to close, they consolidated into the recently-built high school in my town.

Just a few miles east, the county seat of Cumberland, a "metropolis" of 20,000 people, lies in the valley below. It is the site of a ferocious inter-municipality debate: the weather.

Growing up, our neighbors, who enjoy warmer temperatures and less snow due to the elevation difference, were not afforded as many snow days as us lucky ducks in the mountains. When Mother Nature dumped snow on my town, forcing school cancelations, Cumberland's milder conditions often warranted a normal school day, or if they lucked out, a two-hour delay. The ensuing result was mayhem: aggrieved school attendees and their parents took to social media to argue about the weather and direct-Tweet the superintendent of Allegany County Schools. As my sister used to posit in jest, "Ah, Western Maryland: Where We Argue Simple Altitude Difference." Altitude was a way to discriminate and prove superiority in the part of Maryland I come from, which makes sense if you consider an otherwise homogenous population with few other ways to establish difference. Our classmates at the Frostburg high school we attended, Mountain Ridge, even had shirts made to provoke a rival Cumberland school, Fort Hill, that read: "Our ridge tops your hill!"

Cumberland's troubles go far beyond snow-day deprivation, however. Once a thriving industrial city, it is now the poorest municipality in Maryland with an average median income less than half that of the state.[6] Its violent crime rate ranks sixth, and its overdoses are, in part, responsible for the county's status as bearers of the third-highest per capita rate in the state.[7]

What about Appalachia as a whole? For context, here's a brief deep dive into an overview of its historical background and my town's place in it.

Appalachia lacks defined boundaries, but the most common definition is that used by the Appalachian Regional Commission (ARC), created in 1965. The region extends from northern Mississippi to southern New York, tracing the Appalachian Mountains and encompassing all of West Virginia and parts of twelve other states: Alabama, Georgia, Kentucky, Maryland, Mississippi, New York, North Carolina, Ohio, Pennsylvania, South Carolina, Tennessee, and Virginia. Over 25 million people live in the region, primarily in rural communities. The heart of Appalachia is generally thought to lie in the convergence of Eastern Kentucky, Southern West

---

6   Samuel Stebbins, "These are the poorest cities in every state in the US," *USA TODAY*, May 7, 2019.

7   "2018 Crime in the United States: Maryland," *FBI: UCR*; "Unintentional Drug- and Alcohol-Related Intoxication Deaths in Maryland, 2018," *Maryland Department of Health*, May 2019.

Virginia, and Western Virginia—an area that has historically seen the most economic peril.[8]

Appalachia traces much of its lineage to Scots-Irish emigration, particularly Ulster-Scots from present-day Northern Ireland, who arrived in the eighteenth and early nineteenth centuries. With the settlement of the Atlantic Coast, Scots-Irish began pushing westward into the interior backcountry along the spine of the Appalachian Mountains. These were fiercely independent working-class whites, primarily involved in the raw material economy: logging, mining, and later, heavy industry.

By the mid-twentieth century, Appalachia's impoverished communities began to gain the national spotlight. You may remember the famous image of Lyndon Johnson squatting on the front porch of Tom Fletcher's Martin County home as he listened to Fletcher detail the stark reality of life in rural Kentucky. This image was a spark that ignited Johnson's War on Poverty, and with it, the creation of bodies such as the ARC to work on issues afflicting the region. Here we can draw a direct line from the Appalachia's rising national prominence to many of the commonly heard stereotypes about the region: banjo-playing, moonshine-drinking rednecks and hillbillies.

Although these stereotypes may paint a distorted picture of Appalachia as it exists today, the region remains afflicted by a host of serious problems: economic deprivation, health disparities, the opioid epidemic, and environmental degradation, to name a few. The ARC monitors each of the 420 counties included in the Appalachian region, categorizing them based on three indicators: unemployment rate, per capita market income, and poverty rate. These values are

---

8   "The Appalachian Region," *Appalachian Regional Commission.*

then compared to the national average to sort the counties into a rating system that ranges in order of most to least economically depressed: Distressed, At-Risk, Transitional, Competitive, Attainment. Distressed counties rank in the bottom 10 percent nationally, while those that have achieved Attainment have climbed into the top 10 percent nationally. Nearly 20 percent of Appalachia's counties fit into the Distressed category. My county is fortunate enough to be labeled as Transitional, meaning it is in the middle of the pack relative to the others, and has largely avoided the worst economic impacts that have decimated Central Appalachia.[9] However, when you dive deeper, my county's woes become clear.

The ARC has identified four distressed areas within my county. These are pockets that have a "median family income no greater than 67 percent of the US average and a poverty rate 150 percent of the US average or greater."[10] Furthermore, the percentage of those completing college in my county totals less than half the Maryland average—and even lags 5 percent behind Appalachia overall.[11] Per capita income falls below the national average, while both poverty and unemployment rates exceed it.[12] The heart disease mortality rate ranks in the worst quintile nationally, and opioid overdoses have ravaged local communities.[13]

9   "County Economic Status in Appalachia, FY 2020," *Appalachian Regional Commission*.

10 "County Economic Status and Distressed Areas in Appalachia," *Appalachian Regional Commission*

11 "Education—High School and College Completion Rates, 2013-2017: Appalachian Maryland," *Appalachian Regional Commission*.

12 "County Economic Status, Fiscal Year 2020: Appalachian Maryland," *Appalachian Regional Commission*.

13 "Interactive Data," *Creating a Culture of Health in Appalachia: Disparities and Bright Spots*.

Poor, white, uneducated.

In broad strokes, this is the area in which I grew up. The fascinating thing is how little people outside the region seem to grasp its troubles. My current vantage point in college has given me an interesting perspective. Enclosed in my cozy liberal bubble, I'm surrounded by thoughtful, well-intentioned people who care about making the world a better place. They stand for climate justice, advocate for income redistribution, and post about human rights issues on their Facebook feeds. Many want to devote their lives to solving these issues and more. This is all great. I'm proud to go to school with such socially conscious and worldly individuals.

Still, I am struck by how overlooked the issues facing Appalachia continue to be in all of this. It's not malicious or intentional, but Appalachia is woefully misunderstood and forgotten about. It is a region of 25 million people that touches a quarter of our states—and yet, many of my friends can't believe the stories I tell them about what life is like here. They can't fully grasp that real people *actually* believe the Trumpist rhetoric, tune their radios to Rush Limbaugh, and mount campaigns to secede from their own state. Perhaps, in theory, they know that this kind of America exists, out there, *somewhere.* But when you grow up in an isolated liberal haven, attend fancy prep schools, and spend summers on the Cape, you aren't exactly confronted with what your average Joe thinks about the Muslim Ban, how a card-carrying NRA member reacts to gun control legislation, or what a coal miner thinks about the Paris Climate Accords. Why would you?

To many of them, Appalachia is still the photo of Lyndon Johnson on the porch, the dusty miner axing coal by day and downing moonshine by night, the hillbilly living in a trailer home. It's a caricature, one that's been perpetuated over and over again in news, TV, and movies, blending the line between fiction and reality. Through this, Appalachia becomes less of a real, tangible place and more a societal punching bag serving as a convenient source of entertainment. This failure to consider Appalachia is apparent when we wake up confused that 63 million Americans decided to blow up the system and install Trump. We read *New York Times* think-pieces that try to probe the minds of Trump voters in a diner in Ohio. We hear news reports about the "silent majority." *Who are these people*, we think?

What matters, in the end, is not just one's agreement or disagreement on the issues. It's the knowledge that the people behind them exist and an understanding of the pervasiveness of their viewpoints. Yes, alarming secessionist movements are occurring 150 years after the age of Robert E. Lee, but I'm equally concerned about the other half of America that hasn't woken up to it yet, trifling away in insularity. It's keeping a pulse on a group of people you can't cast off no matter how troubling their politics might be. It's a recognition that Appalachia is transitioning, a vast swath of the country trying to find a new identity and chart a new course. An understanding that it is a region with real people facing real problems.

***

Origins are a funny thing. We often concoct stories in our head, making our upbringings seem coherent, natural, and ordinary. When we meet someone new, we mindlessly rehearse our "I'm from X..." intros seemingly without batting an eye. It makes sense that we *make sense* of our upbringings. It's human psychology to bring order to chaos, to construct a linear narrative. To an extent, we all buy into this mindset of collective ignorance, trusting the universe has correctly calibrated our existence and disregarding the fact that in reality, blind luck largely determines the people and places that shape our upbringings.

I often think about this when I hear many of my college peers talk about growing up. Their stories seem to flow. The artsy kid who grew up in a hipster neighborhood in Manhattan. The vehement leftist who grew up among card-carrying socialists in Cambridge. The entrepreneur who grew up among Wall Street traders and hedge funds.

Then there's me—the intensely curious and open-minded progressive who grew up in a land of deer bologna, black smoke-belching diesel trucks, and extreme conservatism. I'm often met with a confused look or a blank stare when I first tell someone I'm from Appalachia, prompting me to follow with a "You know, like *Hillbilly Elegy?*" For most people, this does the trick. "Ah, okay, like redneck country." Then, "Wait—*you* came from *there*? How did that happen?"

This always brings me to tell the story of my parents. My dad grew up in suburban New Jersey in the '60s and '70s. His dad was a Princeton graduate and chemical engineer whose dad's side of the family fled the Pograms in Galicia in the early twentieth century. His mom's side of the family has English ancestry supposedly extending back to the *Mayflower*. My dad was incredibly well-rounded: excelling in three sports, academically dedicated, socially popular, musically inclined. Basketball was his favorite (the apple doesn't fall far from the tree). As he used to exclaim with a toothy grin, New Jersey/New York was the "Mecca" of basketball at that time. Walking down the street, one was bound to find other kids playing pickup, no matter the season, time of day, or weather. Things were competitive. He developed a Jersey grit, a toughness, but also a kind, gentle soul. Always curious, he had an intellectual bent, going on to study psychology and pursue a career in academia.

My mom, meanwhile, grew up outside Hartford, Connecticut. The middle of three sisters, she is of Irish, German, and Scottish heritage and has deep roots in New England on both sides. When I asked her about her family history, she uncovered a handwritten family tree she had constructed for a college class almost forty years ago. Family members dot the Northeastern Seaboard, except for one great aunt who appears to have gone against the grain by moving to the West Coast. My mom's scribbled notes peg her as the one who got away.

My mom dabbled in a number of things growing up, but I happen to think water ballet is the coolest of the bunch. I have learned to not compete with her in any water-based activity. She will kick your butt in the backstroke.

She has always been a selfless doer—constantly taking care of others, putting them above herself, making sure all is well. It comes as no surprise she decided to make a career of it as a social worker, helping out society's most vulnerable. I have always admired her approach. For her, it's just second nature.

My parents met while attending college at the University of New Hampshire in the late '70s. What was the first date for these two hippies? Making granola with ingredients from their local co-op. Or at least that's what they tell my sister and me, which has become a family joke ever since. "Oh, yeah, they were just making granola." It doesn't get much more '70s than that.

Both my parents come from a mental health background. After graduate school, my dad completed his post-doctorate fellowship at Harvard and later worked in New Hampshire, treating patients in a community mental health center, directing a Dartmouth pediatric headache clinic, and teaching at the medical school. My mom also treated patients in social services, focusing on substance abuse. As they began to think about having a family, their calculations changed. As much as my dad enjoyed his career, he sought a better work-life balance. Between his research and professorship duties at Dartmouth, in addition to his counseling work, he was working long hours. He began looking for new opportunities in academia that offered more of an opportunity to be with his kids.

Eventually, he ended up at Frostburg State University in Western Maryland. My parents did not intend for it to be a long-term stop. They had abandoned their Northeast roots, entering an environment wildly different from their previous homes. Looking back, it was quite an unlikely locale, one in which neither really had any connection. However, they took a liking to its rolling mountains, opportunities for hiking, biking, and other outdoor activities, the slow pace of life, lack of traffic, and above all, the chance to devote their attention to raising my sister and me.

So it was that I grew up as an outsider in Appalachia, itself a foreign place to both parental lineages. I often wonder what would have happened had I grown up in an alternate universe, one in which my parents were born and raised in Appalachia; their upbringings and New England roots replaced by a largely insular existence in Western Maryland. Physically sheltered from the world beyond, the mountains acting as bulwarks against change—resisting assimilation to the ways of the people "downstate" in Baltimore and DC. Their lifetime of diverse experiences and accumulated wisdom instead replaced by teachings partially informed primarily by fear and hostility toward outsiders. Their political ideology influenced by the talking heads on Fox News, the Alex Jones-esque conspiracy theorists who sow distrust of objective reality, and the conservative talk radio hosts who launch climate-denying polemics. What then?

Such a hypothetical is hard for me to envision. Entertaining it is a sobering reminder of nature/nurture and our utter powerlessness in the grand scheme of things. It makes me grateful for my parents and instills in me an empathy for the region. Had my parents come from such a background, I would all but certainly be rooted in nativism and xenophobia like many with whom I grew up. I would probably think the Confederate flag is a perfect object to proudly display in my front lawn and I would lambaste the socialists trying to take my guns. Hell, maybe I would have thought Obama to be a secret Muslim. I would not be attending Bowdoin, and I certainly would not be writing this book.

It makes me think of the late David Foster Wallace and his 2005 commencement address at Kenyon College.

> "There are these two young fish swimming along, and they happen to meet an older fish swimming the other way, who nods at them and says, 'Morning, boys, how's the water?' And the two young fish swim on for a bit, and then eventually one of them looks over at the other and goes, 'What the hell is water?'"[14]

---

14   David Foster Wallace, "Transcription of the 2005 Kenyon College Commencement Address—May 21, 2005."

I often felt like the unaccompanied fish, living in the region but experiencing it from an external perspective. Present, but removed. It's a confusing and complicated thing to put words to such an odd existence.

What follows is my attempt.

CHAPTER 2 –

FAMILY

————

The term "family values" always seems to pop up in political discourse. The GOP, in particular, has claimed the supposed mantle of the party of family values dating back to Jerry Falwell's 1980s "Moral Majority," which proclaimed things like abortion, secularism, and the LGBTQ community to be signs of America's moral decay. The key to reversing this decline, said Evangelicals and Reaganites, was the return to the traditional family: i.e. stable two-parent households capable of instilling "virtuous" teachings in their kids. According to them, the family, not the government, knew what was best. As such, family should be central in one's life.

***

The importance of family in daily life was always apparent in Appalachia. Small-town politics were a fact of life. The key to navigating this? Family. Playing time for sports teams? You can bet it will be relevant. Awards and recognitions? Yep. Local elections? Big time. The family name was everything.

It wasn't just that my family differed from the norm. It was the lack of family history, the missing Appalachian roots that rendered us outsiders. It was the fact that all my extended family resided elsewhere—Vermont, Maine, Connecticut, Oregon, Arizona, Colorado, you name it. To me, that was a normal thing. But as I grew up, I began to see how strong the family unit was in my community. Having family far and wide was mostly a foreign phenomenon.

I can't tell you the number of times I had teachers who told classmates, "Oh, I taught your parents, too! And your uncle!" Or the difficulty my sister and I had doing trivial sports team duties—like selling hoagies to raise money—because we pretty much had no one to market them to. I remember buying up all our allotted share, totally defeating the purpose of the sale. Meanwhile, teammates sold to cousins, aunts, uncles, and grandparents galore. There was this sense of dread that washed over me each time team fundraising came around. My sister and I both were multi-sport athletes, so it always felt like we were desperately trying to convince people to buy hoagies or the vaunted Appalachian pepperoni rolls (people were seriously obsessed—look them up) from the local family-run joint. It unintentionally acted as an exercise in reinforcing our outsider status. After all, I did not want to let the team down by being the *one* person who failed to meet my quota and adequately shower the region in hoagie glory. But I mean, really—who the fuck was I going to sell 47 hoagies to?

As silly as this all may sound, it was ostracizing. I look back and chuckle at the insignificance of this whole ordeal in the scheme of things, but it really was the kind of tradition that was a big deal in small-town life. I'm not quite sure how to accurately capture it. In fact, this is a trend my sister and I often joke about when we find ourselves recounting stories like this to college friends unfamiliar with the region. No matter how well we try to articulate it and no matter how much our captive audiences nod in agreement, there is always a layer of misunderstanding cloaked in confused disbelief: e.g. "So... hoagies are like... really important?" We then struggle to find the words to affirm the statement because we ourselves do not quite understand it either. "Well... yes... I mean, it's not really the hoagies on their own merits. They're just... it's just this weird phenomenon... just take my word for it that pepperoni rolls mattered, and they somehow played an outsized role in my upbringing."

Add in the fact that our sports teams rarely ever had more than a day or two off from practice for the holidays (I actually have more days off as a college basketball player than I did for small-town high school sports!). After all, why would you need a break to visit family? They live right down the road! It was like no one really understood that not everyone lived around here. Visiting family was a sacred thing for me. I didn't get to see them all the time, so I cherished the times when I did. When friends said they were just casually heading over to their grandparents' down the street, it always took me a second to grasp how normal and routine it was.

I guess, in a way, I was envious of this arrangement. What it would have been to have felt grounded and immersed in a place that felt familiar. To some extent, I longed to be a part of something bigger, all the while renouncing what such a scenario would look like. It is weird for me to imagine my family being clustered in the same area; generations passing through the same institutions, carrying on local dynasties. Perhaps the fact that my family did not fit this mold actually brought us closer together, a united front operating among established family lineages. If I ever needed to discuss something, my nuclear family was my best bet. Sure, my extended family was a phone call away, but it wasn't as if I could show up to my grandmother's doorstep like many of my peers. In this way, it's almost paradoxical; family was central in my life due to the larger absence of family in my area.

They were the only ones who "got it." My sister especially, was the confidant with whom I could speak my mind, knowing we had a shared experience. We both had small circles of close friends as we came of age, I especially so. Within that, most of our close family friends likewise did not have Appalachian origins.

Don't get me wrong, I was friendly with a lot of people, just not necessarily by choice. For me, friendships really shifted once I hit middle school and high school. As a kid, things were much simpler. I played baseball, soccer, and basketball year-round and many of my friendships revolved around this. The criteria were pretty basic: did this person enjoy shooting hoops? Could we play whiffle ball in my backyard? Check. Friend material. At that age, troubling behaviors I would come to reject as I got older had not even begun to manifest themselves.

By the time I entered high school, however, I naturally started valuing friendships for different reasons as my own sets of morals and values solidified. Of course, the same thing was happening for many of my peers, but our value systems were beginning to greatly diverge. This made things pretty difficult for me at times. I was on a different trajectory and there was little able to bring us together. Even for those with whom I shared a major interest (e.g. basketball), differing fundamental values often made it hard to connect or dissuaded me from even wanting to try.

I know by now this situation may sound like it calls for one of the "let's all have bipartisan civility" platitudes that has become all-too-common in our polarized political environment. "Just because you don't share the same politics doesn't mean you can't be friends!" "You don't have to talk politics!" "Just agree to disagree!" The trouble was the divisions weren't merely about my dislike for small government, the NRA, or a ballot cast for Trump (though disconcerting in and of itself). It was the kind of belief system that often accompanied and anchored this support that was deeply troubling. It was blatant racism, sexism, and homophobia that proved irreconcilable for me. It was a fundamental clash of worldviews to the point where I found it hard to look past things I was hearing in favor of "just being friends." I was not interested in surrounding myself with people who espoused such sentiments.

***

Operating underneath all of this was not just a divergence in fundamental values but a disagreement on a basic set of facts and assumptions about the world. Politically polarized gaps between my peers and me became epistemic chasms. I had to look no further than my Facebook feed to see the onslaught of "alternative facts" pervading the basic idea of what it means to know something. Sure, you don't have to talk politics, but what happens when you exist in not only a different moral hemisphere but a different universe entirely? How do you put politics aside then? Politics becomes less a sectioned-off topic of discussion and more an all-encompassing lens through which to view the world, one that seeps into areas far beyond debates on, say, healthcare or guns.

I get that we all regret things we say and do as we are growing up and figuring ourselves out. I look back and surely feel a tinge of guilt for certain episodes. But beyond the normal trials and tribulations of adolescence, there is an ethical line, one I felt was inexcusably bypassed by my peers on a number of occasions. Trespassing the line often felt like the rule, not the exception.

Did I mention the time in the locker room that teammates, liberally tossing around the N-word, singled me out for not supporting *slavery* because I was, and I quote, "a liberal"? In that moment, it was useless to offer up whatever retort I could find words for. "You don't have to be a liberal to not support slavery" was not going to be changing any minds. I don't know what's worse—the harsh reality that they were only partially joking about their own racist attitudes or the fact that they thought it was acceptable to even joke about slavery in the first place. I remember having to play a game after that, acting like everything was normal and passing them the ball as if I hadn't just heard them trafficking in Klan rhetoric a few minutes prior. May I remind you this whole encounter took place a mere 150 years after the dissolution of the Confederacy? It was moments like this that made my town—within walking distance of the Mason-Dixon—feel a whole lot closer to the Gulf of Mexico.

There's the "coaching" my sister's basketball team received before playing a predominantly black team from Baltimore. One coach assuaged fears by urging aggressiveness against the "big black girls" and "beasts," assuring physicality would be permissible because "it [the black] won't rub off." Horrified at what she was hearing, my sister intervened: "Coach, we don't call ourselves the skinny white girls, why do we have to keep referring to them as 'the big black girls?'" The response? "Shut up, GG, you're the biggest liberal in here."

She somehow kept it together for the remainder of practice and the silence that ensued in the locker room after, subsequently rushing home to recount what happened. This was obviously unacceptable conduct in its own right, but what's worse is that I'm not sure others on the team really batted an eye. Perhaps they were initially taken aback at the way she was called out, but... she *was* the biggest liberal in the gym... *that figures.* I think this ultimately speaks to our existence in the region. It felt like perpetually yelling into the void *THIS IS OUTRAGEOUS AND NO ONE SEEMS TO NOTICE.* My dad later had a meeting with the coach to set the record straight. My sister accepted her coach's apology, but she lost a lot of interest in the team after that and still had to put up with teammates making fun of her about the experience whenever they got the chance. She often expressed to me how it was the one time—out of all the many, many times she had heard inappropriate comments from students and teachers alike—she had decided to say something, and that's what she had been met with. Her strategy, especially by the second half of high school, morphed into one I had previously never seen in my sister: keep your head down, say whatever the people in power wanted to hear, graduate—do whatever you needed to do to be able to one day get the heck out.

And then there are the countless Holocaust jokes made at the lunch table, the racist jabs launched at Obama, the refrains about the "Mexicans taking our jobs" (that one is vile to begin with, let alone when you consider my county's demographic makeup: 90 percent white and 1.9 percent Hispanic or Latino).[15] Of course, much of what I was hearing was a direct recitation of what was being heard at home.

---

15   "QuickFacts, Allegany County, Maryland," *United States Census Bureau.*

All this is to say that my small circle was not for lack of interest or will. My sister and I both were gregarious and extroverted individuals; it simply was not in the cards for the most part. My sister was the more fortunate of the two of us in that she happened to at least be surrounded by a couple of others in her class who were on the same wavelength. They were socially conscious, planned to pursue college (maybe even out of the region), and could likewise generally empathize with the experience. I, on the other hand, did not really experience the same fate with kids in my age range, which could be demoralizing.

The part that stung was the fact that my frustrations were purely a dynamic unique to home. I had friends far and wide elsewhere. Everywhere I went—whether it was the travel basketball teams I competed on or the government programs I participated in—I seemed to develop close friendships and meet other open-minded, curious, and ambitious folks. It took these experiences to certify that which, although sometimes hard to accept in the moment, I always knew to be true: I would eventually find my people. They were out there in the ether beyond our insulated bubble. As my dad always repeated, "You just gotta wait. You're gonna find your tribe."

"Find your tribe" served as the guiding light at the end of the tunnel when I became fed up with racist locker room shenanigans and secessionist Facebook rants and climate change denials. It was affirmed by my sister as she left for college and experienced it firsthand, relaying her epiphanies back home. I remember her calling home after a class, completely ecstatic: "Guess what? I raised my hand and actually shared my true opinion in class today. Like, I said what the little voice in the back of my head was saying, not what I thought everyone wanted to hear. And the weird thing was, people in class actually agreed with me. That has literally never happened! And the professor was so impressed she emailed me after class!"

"Find your tribe" formed the backbone of my college search, the common denominator uniting each of the different schools I visited. I was in a weird state of limbo: waiting for college, not knowing exactly how it would be but knowing it would be exactly what I needed. Once at Bowdoin, I can say I have found thoughtful, bright, and profoundly interesting people. I have found a tribe.

There's still a sort of sadness that hangs over home when I return for a school break and all of the stories wash over me. Home entailed a place of great frustration. Don't get me wrong—I had a great childhood, filled with innumerable happy memories. My parents were always around, and they supported us in everything we did. We took family trips together out West, attended many a Orioles and Wizards game, and spent a lot of time outdoors. We were always comfortable and secure. Looking back, the fact that most of my warm and fuzzy memories center around my family is a testament to our existence in the region. Our bonds were deepened through shared experience. We depended on each other to stay sane and add a note of levity to the situation. It was the family we came back to when my mom received pushback on city council for trying to make the city more inclusive, or when my dad stuck out like a sore thumb at my Little League games rocking Chuck Taylor high-tops and Hawaiian shirts among the sea of other dads sporting Under Armour polos and khaki shorts, or when my sister and I were called out for being dirty liberals. We embraced this collective identity, taking solace in the absurdity of it all. It was sort of funny in a way.

At the same time, there was a guarded element to our existence. Perhaps by now, you can imagine why my family wanted to keep things close, especially politically. If Appalachia was the tinder, we were the liberal spark. Keeping your mouth shut when you didn't *need* to be disclosing things was a way to avoid unnecessary headaches. It was a bad enough sin to be a *liberal*. What other skeletons were in the closet?

Well, there's the time my sister had to map our family's ancestry for a project in her Advanced Placement (AP) Human Geography class. By that point, she had a bad case of senioritis and was soon off to Middlebury College in Vermont. I was finishing eighth grade, gearing up to tackle high school. It was a pretty routine family tree project, but my dad was worried about a sinister underside. His paternal grandfather's side of the family was Jewish, and his dad, while not practicing, was culturally Jewish. What would happen when her classmates stumbled upon the "Wolfman" name held by my ancestors before they assimilated and changed it to Edwards? He insisted my sister not include this piece of the puzzle in her project for fear of how it would be interpreted in our ultra-conservative community—regardless of the fact that we did not practice, could barely be considered culturally Jewish in our own right, and certainly did not identify as such. The rationale always was, "Your brother still has to get through this place." I remember her scrambling to replace the blank spot left on her poster board after my dad made her peel it off the morning it was due.

Yes, it is important to stand up for what is right (like when my dad confronted my sister's basketball coach), embrace your identity, and refuse to be beholden to what others think. My parents were living proof of this. But it was just as, if not more, important to understand the delicate balance of knowing when to pick your battles. This wasn't exactly the ideal environment to reveal Jewish heritage—in fact, I can't remember knowing a single Jew in my town growing up. They only made their way into my life via peers' Holocaust jokes or the occasional epithet muttered by a classmate to express disdain (Frustrated by a teacher assigning homework? Kid misses the ball during kickball in gym class? "He's such a Jew."). My dad simply did not want to make my life any more complicated than it had to be as I navigated high school by revealing this aspect of our identity—no matter how far removed it was in our history. In retrospect, what an insane episode in my family's life! Not to mention that at Bowdoin, Judaism is not only accepted, but it's also celebrated. It feels like *everybody* is Jewish, a complete 180 from what I experienced at home.

My family tiptoed the line of being secure in our identity while being careful to not overdo it, knowing full well this was not where we could be welcomed with open arms. It's like we were tenants in an Airbnb. Yeah, the place was ours for the time being, but it wasn't *ours*. And we definitely weren't going to be throwing a rager in the place.

For many others in the local community, family took on a whole new meaning. Preserving the family meant staying close to home and perpetuating its entrenchment in the region. Family became closely intertwined with place. The region itself acted as a bubble in preserving the region's ways and traditions. In other words, the same sort of guardedness to which my family resorted was not always necessary—*this* was the place being guarded against outsiders. When I consider the tight-knit nature of family life in Appalachia, it leads me to think deeply about the pervasiveness of xenophobia in my community. I sometimes wonder if the extreme love and protection of one's family and way of life manifests itself as a fear of outsiders. It's almost as if people's apparent hostility toward those who aren't from the region is not as much intolerance as it is a coping mechanism born out of intense devotion to the insular group—the group that has always been there right in front of their eyes.

To be clear, I absolutely do not condone the bigoted attitudes so commonplace among my peers. Beyond these explicit comments, I'm wondering about the general predisposition to wariness toward outsiders in the region—or, at least, the nepotism toward locals. Why did it feel like my family was not met with open arms? At face value, we were just like many families with whom I grew up: white, middle-class, hard-working.

For all the differences between us, we both shared a love for our families. The surrounding circumstances meant this love was sometimes expressed in different ways. I've never felt a deep attachment to the region, partly due to the lack of family roots and partly due to the nature of growing up as an outlier. Yet, when I try to put myself in the shoes of one with an opposite story, I imagine I, too, would be defensive, quick to protect the region and my loved ones from "outside" influence. Appalachia has seemingly always been ridiculed and mocked for being "inbred" and "backward," its hillbillies and *Deliverance* banjo scenes becoming de facto regional symbols for external audiences.

I imagine the commercialized image is, in a way, comforting for audiences outside the region. It gives them something to which they can feel superior. Appalachians carry the weight of all this baggage with them, baggage I do not necessarily think has always weighed me down in the same way. Their identity is intricately intertwined with the region, a place that can bring deep pride but deep insecurity. From this perspective, I can somewhat understand the instinctual need to defend the family honor and that of the region as a whole. Once again, this absolutely does not excuse bigotry and intolerance, but rather, it may explain some of the reasons my family's existence felt so out of place at times. We didn't feel the need to defend the honor—we were the home intruders warranting its defense.

PART 2:

THE OUTLIER

CHAPTER 3 –

WALK OUT OR WALK IN?

_____

We can feel the support from all over the country and the energy hasn't died down. Keep the momentum going.

I glanced down at my phone, seeing the text message slide across the top of the screen. *This is why I'm doing it,* I thought with a smile. It was March thirteenth. The next morning, I would be spearheading a class walkout at ten a.m. and delivering a speech in accordance with the National School Walkout, a movement to honor the victims of the mass shooting in Parkland, Florida that happened the month prior. The text was from a Parkland native, a friend I had just met the week before while attending a government program in DC. There, with tears running down his face, he told me how much it meant to him and the rest of his classmates to see students around the country join them in standing up to the NRA and apathetic politicians. When I arrived back home, I knew I had to do something.

Previously, I was a little hesitant to organize a walkout at my school—not because of a personal disagreement with the cause but rather, due to the circumstances of my local environment. Gun and hunting culture is deeply entrenched in Appalachia. I'm not just talking about a belief in the second amendment. I'm talking about guns as a cultural pillar that manifests itself in an in-your-face kind of way. Deer heads on the basement walls during sleepovers at friends' houses; couples wearing camouflage dresses and tuxes at prom (complete with muzzleloaders for props in pictures); entire sections of the local newspaper devoted to displaying pictures of classmates proudly holding up carcasses of the eight-point buck they bagged last weekend. *Everybody* hunted. There were always school absences en masse on the first day of hunting season each year, even among teachers. Friends' parents were card-carrying members of the NRA. Hillary was going to take everybody's guns, so I was told.

Politically, I had always been engaged, eager to debate, and hungry for stimulating discourse, but I didn't always have a place to direct it in my conservative town. Sometimes I couldn't help but interject and correct the record when I would overhear racist jokes at the lunch table or conspiracy theories about Obama's birth certificate. Until senior year, though, I primarily kept personal opinions to myself when around others outside of family and close family friends. What was the point? I was rarely, if ever, going to change anybody's mind. If anything, *I* was the one who needed to be converted and purged of my progressive beliefs, in their eyes.

My county voted 72 percent for Donald Trump, second only behind our neighboring county for the highest percentage in Maryland. Moreover, few of my peers were particularly interested in having political conversations and keeping an open mind. Holding progressive views—or for that matter, simply failing to toe the Tea Party line—was isolating; feeding into it only meant further solidifying my outlier status and adding fuel to the fire of small-town politics. There was constant tension. I wanted to express myself and abide by the political courage teachings I had soaked up in JFK's *Profiles in Courage*—after all, what good are your values if you do not act upon them in the face of opposition?—but doing so meant digging deeper into the quicksand. I was definitely wary of stirring the pot too much. We all were. Looking back, I don't really know if it would have made much of a difference. Everyone already knew my family's MO.

It was incredibly frustrating to balance staying true to my political and moral convictions with the need to stay quiet due to the stifling environment. Yet, by senior year—and senior spring especially—I was a lame duck student. My time in Appalachia was winding down, and I was soon headed off to a private liberal arts college in New England, the antithesis of home. There, I would soon enough "find my tribe" as my dad would say. My high school sports career—and the politics accompanying it—had finished. I had nothing to lose by this point if I were to fully speak my mind. It was time to channel *Profiles in Courage* in my small way.

So, as I headed back home from my time in DC with my newfound Parkland friends, I decided action was necessary. I began organizing a gun violence walk out with a few sympathetic individuals in my school. We convened a meeting with the school administration, and unsurprisingly, our challenge to the right to bear arms was not met with open arms. They were unsupportive of us walking out of the school. To put it bluntly, some of the reasoning was ludicrous. They cited concerns about safety (ironic given the nature of the protest was to vouch for gun reforms to keep students safe in schools) and the expected temperature outside that day (cold, just like *every* other winter day in our snowy, mountaintop town). One administration official even mentioned that if we were to rally outside, people were likely to be distracted by "birds and other things." Clearly, the million students who were projected to walk out across the country would manage to deal with squawking crows, wind chills, and other "barriers." I found their unfounded objections entirely unacceptable.

Word travels quickly in a small town. Soon the county superintendent released a memo saying any walkout plans would need to be modified to be a "walk-in" (i.e. people leave class for an assembly in the auditorium instead of leaving the school). Further, the walkout was framed as almost entirely apolitical. Instead of acting as a rebuke of the gun lobby and the indifferent politicians offering "thoughts and prayers," the walk-in was allowed so long as it was a memorial for Parkland. Of course, I wanted to honor those lost in the horrific shooting, but to separate gun reform activism from the walkout would be a disgrace to both the movement's founders—who explicitly called on Congress to pass gun control legislation—and those who died at the hands of gun violence not just in Parkland but around the nation.

I still don't know what was behind the rationale of the administration and the school board. Perhaps it was personal disagreement with the ideology behind the walkout, or maybe a recognition of how they would be perceived by the ultra-conservative community if it were to take place. All I know is it felt like only in an area as backward as mine would the decision transpire without provoking significant pushback. Hearing the walk-in news was a punch to the gut. It felt like a perfect concoction that brought out those aspects of home I most despised: the classic small-town failure to look beyond our pinpoint on the map to consider something bigger; the obstinate retreat into the regressive mindset of "this is the way it always has been, so this is the way it has to be"; the warped circular logic put forth in defense of the decision that was made.

As I coordinated with friends around the country who were organizing their own respective walkouts, they could not believe what was happening with my school. Despite my frustration, I needed to compromise. It was either a diluted walk-in or nothing at all. Ultimately, I figured that although the optics of actually walking out of the school were desirable, I could achieve many of the same goals through the walk-in. I know JFK lauded the political courage of those who demonstrated "unyielding devotion to absolute principles."[16] This would have to be political courage sprinkled with a dash of acquiescence to the whims of squawking administrators and their squawking crows.

***

Keep the momentum going.

As I glanced at my friend's text message on the morning of the fourteenth, I felt reassured and emboldened. I was anxious about how the event would be received, especially given that I had prepared a speech that strongly advocated for gun reform and called out the school system for being unsupportive of the original walkout idea. His text reminded me of why I was doing it.

Much to my surprise, at ten a.m., hordes of classmates began filing out of classrooms en route to the auditorium. People were really walking out! In Appalachia! Those who chose not to participate in the walk-in were instructed to report to the cafeteria. By the time I took the stage, I noticed

---

16   John F. Kennedy, *Profiles in Courage* (New York: Harper Collins, 2006), 19.

the auditorium was filled. Roughly half of the school sat before me, a much larger turnout than I had expected. As I closed my remarks, I urged my peers to register to vote at a registration drive I had orchestrated outside the auditorium. Close to forty students became new voters that day. Granted, many of them registered as Republicans, precisely who had been stonewalling any hope of progress on gun reform legislation in Washington. Regardless, I was encouraged by the sight of more young people becoming involved in the civic process and grateful to have had the opportunity to contribute in my small way to inspiring youth activism. I learned that even amidst non-ideal circumstances in an unfavorable environment, progress was, indeed, possible.

It was only after the speech that I began to see a stream of Facebook posts from those who objected to the walk-in. Dozens of people decked out in their most visible NRA attire had a show of solidarity in the cafeteria during the event—a reverse walk-in of sorts. Given a cause that seemed so easy to rally around, I was disheartened to see this happen. One would think school safety would be paramount to school students, especially given the events in Parkland and other schools around the country. If a school shooting that left 17 students dead didn't shock all students into action, what would? This was a clear lesson for me: although progress is possible even among usually unreceptive audiences, there is a cap. Appalachia would budge a little if nudged, but its limits were clear. Some values were simply too entrenched in the culture to shed.

Nonetheless, I was proud of myself for taking the initiative to be bold, speak out, and mobilize. My outlier status paradoxically reaped benefits—benefits I am not sure I would have gained had I grown up in a community with fewer barriers to assimilation. Appalachia was inculcating in me confidence, self-assurance, and thick skin as a byproduct of its conservative nature. I was learning it was okay to walk against the grain, if not to walk out of the school.

CHAPTER 4

ON THE CAMPAIGN TRAIL

────

When I was a kid, I would sometimes tag along with my mom during her door-to-door canvassing efforts for city council in my town. My mom, perhaps thinking the sight of a cute little kid could only serve to benefit her electoral prospects, was happy to involve me in her campaign. What better way to assuage the fears of conservative voters confronted with a progressive woman at their doorstep than by appointing me de facto campaign manager? We were a tandem duo of sorts: my mom did all the important work—talking to voters, explaining her platform, asking for support, etc.—and I did what I deemed at the time to be equally important: placing signs into front yards to ensure the most neighborhood visibility. For a young kid going through a massive construction phase (I was absolutely obsessed with backhoes, dump trucks, and anything related to building), there was nothing better than getting to hammer a sign into a front lawn.

Campaigning was fun. My job was simple: Mom gave the pitch to the voter and if things went well, she gave the okay for me to grab a sign and hammer away. Granted, campaigning wasn't always as fun for her. She loved going door-to-door to talk to voters and hear about their concerns, but with that exposure came great vulnerability. Each house is a wild card and you never know what you're going to get. Critics, commenders, lecturers, interrogators, you name it—all using that two-minute span on their doorstep as their soapbox for the evening. Add in the fact this is local politics, with all its eccentricities, and *voilà*. As you can guess, my mom has heard it all throughout the years. The streetlights are too bright, the streetlights are too dim, the snowplows aren't running enough, the snowplows are blocking my driveway. You get the picture. Campaigning is an exercise in perseverance.

Sometimes, you know exactly what you're going to get as you walk up to ring the doorbell. Perhaps their existing yard signage gives it away. Obama sign? Yes! Confederate flag? Not so promising. There are more subliminal signals as well. Perhaps the sight of an organic garden, a Prius in the driveway, or solar panels on the roof. All signs of potentially welcoming territory.

Approaching one particular house, my mom was quickly able to infer she likely wouldn't be seen in the most favorable light. She knew the political leanings of the inhabitants but decided to keep an open mind and give it a shot anyway in the off-chance she was able to win a supporter.

My mom began to give her standard pitch but was quickly interrupted. "Oh, I can't vote for you! You're *with the college!*"—implying that my dad's professorship at the local university was somehow an elitist sin.

I started to think this was not going to be a yard into which I would be proudly hammering a sign.

Taken aback, my mom calmly replied, "No, actually, I'm not with the college. My husband is with the college, but I'm not sure why that is important. We chose to move here and raise our children here. I'm running because I care about this community, and I think I can represent it well."

A few aspects of this interaction are particularly telling. The "college" is actually a university, a name change that occurred in the late '80s. As my mom later told me, "If they called it the 'college,' I knew they were locals. If they called it 'university,' I knew they usually weren't from here." To continually refer to it as a "college" thirty years later is indicative of a nostalgia for times gone past and a disillusionment with change.

***

Once a booming industrial center during the early part of the twentieth century, my area has since experienced a free fall. Coal, once the epicenter of the regional economy, has been replaced by newer, cleaner, and more efficient forms of energy. Major manufacturing plants have closed their doors and shipped elsewhere. People who have become disenchanted with the perpetual downward cycle of change have abandoned ship, leading to a rapidly hollowing out population. Once the second most populated city in Maryland behind Baltimore, Cumberland (the county seat) is now experiencing population levels that haven't been seen since 1900.[17]

From this perspective, I understand the resistance to change and can empathize with the deep-seated urge to hold onto the way it used to be. However, for my mother to

17   "Census of Population and Housing, 1900," *U.S. Census Bureau.*

be singled out as having been associated with the "college" speaks to a wider trend among the populace. I continue to be mystified by the cognitive dissonance displayed in my mom's campaign encounter with this man. How could one possibly not support the college? The college is the lifeblood of my town. It is the antidote to the issues afflicting the area, not a cause. It keeps the town humming economically, socially, and culturally—acting not just as a place of employment (the second largest in the county), but also as an alluring draw for speakers, events, concerts, etc. One must look no further than the summertime to see the stark reality of a college town devoid of college students. Main Street feels empty, its small businesses anxiously waiting for the return of a new semester.

Without the college, my town has no anchor. As coal's influence has waned, there is a palpable loss of regional identity. The college fills this gap. No longer can the area take pride in exporting its prized commodity around the world; so prized, in fact, that Western Maryland's coalfields used to power US Navy Fleets and White Star Line transatlantic steamers—maybe even the *Titanic* itself. Coal lying deep in these hills made its way to traders in South America, the Far East, and beyond. Today, aside from a few mines still in operation, abandoned mine shafts and reclamation projects shroud these heroics from view, reminding us that coal's fate has gone the way of the *Titanic*. To have an institution of higher learning in our small town is to have a new legacy on which to rest your laurels.

Moreover, for many, the college is one of the few institutions capable of acting as a vehicle to a better life. The social mobility so ubiquitously sought after in my economically-deprived area rests squarely on its educational infrastructure. Even if one does not appreciate the college on its intellectual merit, I find it hard to reconcile bashing the very institution essential for lifting the region out of poverty.

My mom's encounter likewise struck me for a different reason. The man's comment insinuated that my family was cloaked in some sort of out-of-touch elitism due to our college association. It did not matter that my parents were middle-class individuals working hard just like he was. Or that my dad was definitely not some holier-than-thou academic solely immersing himself in scholarly circles (remember: this is a guy who was active year-round in the community coaching all of my sister's and my sports teams growing up and who was ironically recognized by the college itself for his community service initiatives). Yet in some way, my dad's job as a professor barred us from being *real* Appalachians.

I have to chuckle when entertaining this thought in my mind given the history of the university. It wasn't founded by world-traveling cosmopolitans, leading intellectuals, or the bourgeoisie. Rather, its origins lie in the collective efforts of the local working class; it was founded in large part by coal miners who plunked coins into a collective bucket after coming up from the mines at the end of the day to ensure their kids did not share the same fate. In this sense, the college is the very essence of "real" Appalachia—the physical embodiment of those looking for a better life.

***

I recall the story of my mom's canvassing encounter now because it speaks to a trend that has baffled me for as long as I can remember. There are very real feelings of disillusionment by my peers in Appalachia. The region is largely neglected by the ruling class, contributing to a perpetuating cycle of poverty and discontent with the prevailing order. People feel alienated, exploited, disenfranchised, and deprived of political and economic power—feelings that manifested themselves in the 2016 election and subsequent aftermath. I can fully understand these visceral feelings. Yet, I can't grasp the ways in which they manifest themselves. Disdain for higher education: a force to reverse the region's deepening economic woes. Generational support for the GOP: a party hell-bent on passing 1.5 trillion-dollar tax cuts for the wealthy, while doing little for the working folks who have experienced an economic downturn in the wake of coal's demise. Anger channeled into votes for Donald Trump: a man woefully out-of-touch with Appalachia economically, socially, culturally, and in just about every other regard. Contempt for immigrants "taking" jobs: when automation and trade agreements are the real culprits, and my county is about as non-diverse as it gets.

It is true the system has failed Appalachia. Yet, Appalachians have also failed Appalachia. Shunning the very institutions that can reverse the trend just further perpetuates the cycle. Supporting these institutions rendered my family outsiders. Yes, we were *with the college.* My parents cared about the community and wanted it to prosper. It could be difficult to let that desire shine through, however. As you'll see in the next chapter, difficult might be an understatement…

CHAPTER 5 –

CITY COUNCIL

———

"Who would vote for someone who has a toe ring?"

It was sometime in the early-2000s and my mom was a hopeful future member of the city council. As the story goes, she wore Birkenstocks to a meet-the-candidate forum, committing the ultimate crime of exposing her modest toe rings for the world to see. They weren't much, just two simple, inconspicuous pieces of jewelry—we're not talking major bling here—but I guess it was enough to stir up public resentment among one constituent in my small town. My mom must have done poorly among the anti-open toe shoes demographic in the next election.

It was a minor interaction, really; one my mom recalls now with a still-bewildered chuckle. "What did my toe ring have to do with my ability to do the job?" she posited on a recent phone call. I joked back that if Birkenstocks are a no-go, that dooms the electoral prospects of all my college classmates. The reason I tell my mom's toe ring story now is because it is a microcosm of her experience holding elected office in a place where she was often perceived to be a threat to the status quo.

***

My town's city council consists of a mayor and four commissioners who hold voting and legislative powers. My mom served for eight years as the Commissioner of Public Works. In this role, she was responsible for overseeing the operation of city services, including garbage collection, street sweeping, snow removal, the sewage system, and the city's infrastructure. I always admired the relationships my mom had with many of the employees she oversaw. Picture a group of big, burly guys running the snowplow and my mom bantering and overseeing the crew. They always had a funny back and forth and a healthy mutual respect. I think the guys respected my mom for being a woman in charge of an ultra-masculine space. Plus, she baked them all cookies during the holidays, which never hurt. In addition, she served on the board of the Maryland Municipal League (MML), a non-profit association created to foster collaboration between cities and advocate for their common interests at the state and federal levels.

For the majority of the time she spent on the council, she was in the minority as a female progressive who is not originally from the area. As she puts it, "I served with the good ole boys." In many ways, the frustrations and challenges my mom experienced in her time on city council mirrored my own. I'm not sure I always knew it at the time, but as I've gotten older, I've come to see how my mom embraced her own status as an outlier within city politics. I greatly admire her persistence despite frequently receiving unfair and unwarranted criticism. Her willingness to speak her mind and advocate for what's right in the face of vehement opposition has influenced me to stand up for what I believe in despite potential pushback.

I remember one time my mom put forth a proposal to enter my town into an initiative called the Partnership for Working Toward Inclusive Communities, a program of the National League of Cities. The move was largely symbolic, asking communities to "pass a resolution reaffirming your community's commitment to promoting inclusion; and to proudly display a sign that serves as a daily reminder that your community is working toward a better future for all its citizens."[18] The proclamation was simply a first step, one that publicly acknowledged the city was committed to creating a welcoming community atmosphere. It could complement the smattering of church signs that confront you when you enter town (remember *Frostburg Churches Welcome You?*). Other cities and towns in the tri-state area had already taken the pledge.

This time, however, the proposal was met with fierce opposition. The council voted it down with my mom casting the sole yes vote. The bar had been set so low and yet, the city still failed to surpass it. My mom was incredulous. She recently dug up the newspaper article detailing the vote's blockage: *By 4-1 vote, Frostburg leaders defeat inclusive community concept... Councilwoman 'blown away.'* She's quoted: "All the partnership does is affirm in a public way the very simple thing, that we are an inclusive community. There is no downside at all."[19]

The reasoning for voting against it was, quite frankly, preposterous. One common refrain was "Oh, we don't need that, we're already inclusive," somehow implying the town had no more work to do. As one of my mom's fellow council

---

18 James C. Hunt, letter to author's mother, Feb. 1, 2006.

19 Michael A. Sawyers, "By 4-1 vote, Frostburg leaders defeat inclusive community concept," *Cumberland Times-News,* September 27, 2006.

members chimed in the article, "If it ain't broke, don't fix it." Racism? Boom. Solved. Just like that. Cue the Staples "That was easy!" button.

It's worth noting that my town isn't exactly a thriving multi-cultural hotspot. It owes much of the little diversity it has to the local university. I could pretty much count on two hands the students of color with whom I graduated.

Then you have the mayor, who quipped that "Officially proclaiming the city to be an inclusive community would be a confession that it is not one already." Ah, yes, as MLK famously said, "Alright, guys, I'm done with this whole march thing. That would mean acknowledging that progress can be made." The most ironic part of this backward logic was the fact that my town proudly labeled itself the "Mountain City." Banners lining Main Street exclaimed *Mountain Maryland Welcomes You!* Is this a damning acknowledgment that we used to be a flat hellscape devoid of mountains?

If the "we're already inclusive" talking point wasn't enough, one community member noted completely unrelated concerns about "illegal immigrants… invading" the country and cited the preponderance of "Mexicans" spotted at a nearby state park as a troubling development. He then insinuated that by joining the inclusive partnership, Frostburg was on track to be a "shelter for illegal aliens."[20] Not to be outdone, he followed this up with a scathing op-ed in our local newspaper: *Preamble better welcome sign in Frostburg than 'liberal slogan.'* He directly called out my mom, saying, "Secular progressives like Commissioner Keller drive their agendas literally down our throats with these smear tactics. What I want to see is that the Public Work Commissioner is

---

20   Ibid.

doing her job as a commissioner and not fanning the flames of public sentiment."[21]

Remember, this all started with an innocent proposal to publicly affirm that the city is a welcoming and inclusive environment. At most, this involved putting up a sign. My mom knew she wasn't dealing with a community brimming with social justice advocates receptive to broad social change. She figured this might be a doable first step given the surrounding political environment. Even then, her actions were publicly labeled a "smear campaign." Incredible.

Side note: I also just have to mention the alternative sign slogan raised by the author in his op-ed. He declares, "'We the people of the United States of America,' is the most inclusive statement of government known to mankind,"—conveniently neglecting to mention this phrase was literally written by slave owners.

Despite the political headwinds encountered by my mom, she continued to speak up for what she believed in during her tenure. She faced other political fights, particularly when it came to matters of environmentalism. Her efforts to establish basic environmental initiatives—like curbside recycling, for instance—received major pushback. It actually wasn't until after she finished her eight-year term that curbside recycling became a city service.

Even more troubling, when gas company salesmen approached City Hall looking for lucrative fracking deals, my mom was oftentimes the lone voice of reason. This was a time when little was known about fracking's impacts on groundwater and very few regulations were in place to rein it

---

21 Bernard W. Miltenberger, "Preamble better welcome sign in Frostburg than 'liberal slogan,'" *Cumberland Times-News,* Oct 3, 2006.

in. *Gasland* was one of the few efforts just beginning to sound the public alarm. Not to mention that one of the proposed fracking sites ran right through the reservoir that provides the drinking water for my town and other local municipalities. As my mom put it, "If I hadn't opened my mouth, I felt like we would have immediately signed on the dotted line without even knowing what was happening. I couldn't believe what felt like utter lack of regard that we would so easily sell ourselves without knowledge of regulations or impact on our water supply. To me, that was outlandish."

Or there's the criticism she faced for her role on the Maryland Municipal League (MML); she supposedly spent too much time "downstate" instead of focusing on our own community—criticism that sometimes originated from many of the same folks who decried that Western Maryland was underrepresented and forgotten about in Annapolis. This is ironic, of course, given the whole point of MML was to facilitate collaboration between municipalities and make our town's concerns known at the state level. My mom's involvement in amplifying our voice downstate generated ire from the same people who said we didn't have a voice downstate! She was coincidentally going to bat for a group of people that included some of the Western Maryland secessionists who griped about under-representation.

Sometimes it just felt like my mom could not win, no matter how reasonable and well-intentioned she tried to be. Her path makes me cynical about the prospects for change in Appalachia. Nevertheless, through it all, I'm left inspired by the way she was able to function within this realm despite the resistance she faced. She continually worked with many with whom she disagreed and coolly operated within a largely male-dominated space. It speaks to her grit, toughness, and composure. It speaks to her willingness to compromise when necessary but her unwillingness to sacrifice her values in the face of opposition.

It makes me think once again of JFK's book and the time in high school I submitted an essay for the nationwide *Profiles in Courage* Essay Contest. Drawing on the examples outlined in Kennedy's book, the task was to write about a public official who demonstrated an act of political courage by taking a stand for the public good despite obstacles in their way. At the time, I wrote about former Rutland, Vermont, mayor Chris Louras, who faced intense opposition from constituents for his decision to accept refugees fleeing war-torn Syria. I admired Louras's choice to go against the grain. I still do. But if I had to do it over again, I would have written about my mom.

I feel incredibly grateful for the example my mom set—and her toe rings, of course. Wearing a toe ring in Appalachia is quite the act of political courage, after all.

PART 3:

REFLECTIONS

CHAPTER 6 –

FISH IN A POND

—

Given my family's background, I have always felt like an outsider in Appalachia. I wouldn't identify as Appalachian, nor would I expect others to bestow this title upon my family. Some of the rationale is obvious—my family strayed from the norm politically, socially, and culturally. Yet, even deeper than these categories lies a fundamental difference in the lens through which I viewed my life trajectory.

Both my parents went to graduate schools, attaining terminal degrees in their fields. From a young age, the expectation was for my sister and me to do the same. They were never overly demanding or intent about forcing us onto a particular path, but they definitely pushed us to excel. My parents left it open for my sister and me to dabble in different activities. They actively exposed us to new ideas, places, and people and encouraged us to challenge ourselves (e.g. entering essay contests, free-throw shooting competitions, geography bees, and much more). My dad and I spent endless hours together on the basketball court, perfecting the daily workout we had down to a science. We spent the summers traversing US National Parks (my sister and I will have you know we are Junior Rangers in close to forty of them), taking in historic sites, and crisscrossing America's sweaty gyms from Georgia to Vermont for my busy travel basketball schedule. At home, we were introduced to the soul of Motown and Stax Records, the protest chants of Afrobeat, and the psychedelia of the Grateful Dead—all staples of the eclectic musical education my dad passed on to us. My parents encouraged us to learn and experience everything we possibly could about the world.

My parents structured their entire lives around us. Their kids were their focal point. My dad sacrificed his previous professorship position at Dartmouth to achieve a better work-life balance, and my mom paused her professional career in social work to raise us at home. They never missed games, concerts, or ceremonies—in fact, my dad coached all of our sports teams growing up. The grand vision was for us to emerge as well-rounded, sensitive, thoughtful, and worldly individuals capable of thinking critically, caring about the common good, and tackling any challenges to which we set our sights. I internalized this mindset at a young age, something I became increasingly aware of as I got older. The fact my sister and I had the encouragement to strive for excellence academically, athletically, and in extracurricular endeavors is a testament to the admirable approach my parents took in raising us. I feel incredibly grateful to have had such backing at home. It was built into my upbringing that not only would I attend college one day, but I would be leaving the area, experiencing the world, and setting my sights high.

My sister's and my ambitious worldview clashed with the reality of Appalachia on a number of occasions. For the majority of our peers, leaving the area was never really a thought or real possibility. Economic conditions undoubtedly played a role in this dynamic. For many, however, there was no desire to leave, not just for college, but ever.

It often manifested itself as a total lack of regard for what lay "beyond" and an unwillingness to venture out. There is nothing inherently wrong with this, but it was suffocating to be immersed in this environment. It was the high school teacher who, after hearing my sister was going to college in Vermont, asked her if it was in Canada (not as a joke—he really wasn't sure) and marveled at her internship experience in "CHILL-ee!" (i.e. Chile, the country, not the restaurant chain that microwaves your food and is the subject of coronavirus re-open protests by disgruntled, 2-for-$25 deal-deprived Americans nationwide). It was the classmate who thought Kansas was a fictitious place because of *The Wizard of Oz* and the kid in my AP Language class junior year who, when it was my turn to ascend through the high school ranks, asked if Vermont was part of Massachusetts, and thus, did my sister go to school in Boston? Or, it was when I began my own college search, homing in on schools along the Northeastern Seaboard, I received the question, in earnest: Is New England a country?

For many, college may or may not be an option. In the chance it is, the local community college or Frostburg State are strong bets. "Going away" for school meant attending West Virginia University an hour west or *maybe* the University of Maryland a couple of hours east. I don't say this to paint my sister and myself on a pedestal relative to others but rather to capture the nature of growing up as outliers in the region. We often found it difficult to connect with others outside the nuclear family—our values, goals, and future paths fundamentally diverged from the norm. It seems like no coincidence that our closest family friends in the area were likewise not Appalachians themselves.

The school's guidance counseling service funneled kids into local colleges, not elite institutions. There is, of course, nothing wrong with attending smaller, local colleges; however, my sister and I often felt trapped, enveloped in a collective mindset vastly different than the one bred at home. The knowledge, or lack thereof, pertaining to opportunities that existed outside the area bubble was largely non-existent—even among those in positions of authority. Few, if any, teachers or staff at my school knew of the selective, elite New England Small College Athletic Conference (NESCAC) schools—liberal arts institutions my sister and I would later end up attending. I remember going into the guidance office, only to leave a few minutes later, realizing I was the one guiding the counselor through the prospective school profiles. I was halfway convinced he thought Colby College specialized in cheese making. I guarantee you I have heard every pronunciation of "Bowdoin" imaginable. My sister has been unironically asked on multiple occasions if her alma mater, Middlebury, was a community college.

After returning home one summer from interning at Goldman Sachs in Salt Lake City (That's a whole other story. I joke it's like if Al Gore decided to work at Exxon Mobil—sorry, sis), she would bump into someone on the street and strike up a conversation. At the mention of Goldman Sachs, she was often met with a blank stare, or an empty "Ohhh" and quick change in conversation. One time, she fielded the question: "Goldman Sachs—is that a department store?" *Yes, I flew out to Utah to work at Old Navy. It's not like it is one of the most powerful institutions in the world or anything,* she thought to herself. I'm sorry, but did you miss the Great

Recession? We're talking about one of the globe's largest entities, flush with more cash flowing in and out of its coffers than the GDPs of entire countries.

To be fair, I cannot entirely fault the school administrators, guidance counselors, or even random locals for their unfamiliarity with the college or "department store" in question. This is not Phillips Exeter we are talking about; my school is about the last thing from a pipeline for elite colleges. The area at large is not exactly the center of the economic world. I do not know of anybody from my town in recent memory, save for a friend of my sister's, who even applied to an Ivy or NESCAC, let alone attended one. For that matter, I know of four or five other people in my graduating class of close to 200 who attended college outside of the tri-state area (i.e. Maryland, West Virginia, and Pennsylvania).

Now, of course, college—not to mention the small liberal arts college experience—is not for everybody. And that's okay! With all of this in mind, it makes sense that counselors were not aware of the NESCACs. It's simple supply and demand and there was literally no demand. However, it speaks to the larger point: in the case of high school officials, having an understanding of the college and career landscape is precisely your job. Perhaps there would be more demand if students were made aware of the options that exist in the world, inspired to pursue new paths, and not herded into a certain lifestyle.

I recall one anecdote in which the school invited a UPS employee to talk to my sister's AP Human Geography class about career options. Once again, there is nothing wrong with this. Working at UPS is desirable for many people, and I have great respect for the hardworking folks who earn a living in their profession. But if there is one group of kids at the school who may be involved in pursuing other career paths—especially with a nudge from guidance counselors or teachers—this is the batch of kids! These are the high achievers challenging themselves with an AP class, many of them soon headed to college. Furthermore, while the Armed Services Vocational Aptitude Battery (ASVAB) test was administered class-wide in my school every year without fail (I'm pretty sure it was mandatory), the SAT and ACT remained optional. This fact further reinforces what J. D. Vance notes in *Hillbilly Elegy*: joining the military is virtually the only way to escape the cycle of poverty in places like Appalachia.[22]

I absolutely do not intend for any of the things I explained to this point to come across as elitist or patronizing; I am merely expressing my personal experience and the frustrations and oddities that came with it. Kids from my region are presented with extremely limited options for their futures, if any. I feel very fortunate to have had two highly educated, well-traveled, AARP-aged parents (that last one was often embarrassing at the time—they were seriously 50 when I was in elementary school and a good 10-15 years older than most of my peers' parents) who exposed us to what was out there and provided us with a perspective on life. They were the ones who acted as our guidance counselors and teachers and tour guides and distillers of wisdom at large. Without them, I would have been lost.

By the same token, the stark dichotomy between my family and Appalachia as a whole rendered my sister and me big fish in a small pond. Although we excelled academically, athletically, and in other endeavors, our surrounding

---

22   J. D. Vance, *Hillbilly Elegy: A Memoir of a Family and Culture in Crisis,* (New York: Harper Collins, 2016).

environment was not suited to our ambitions. There was not an abundance of like-minded peers to accompany us in our upbringing, to challenge us, to share our worldview. Our high school wasn't littered with vibrant clubs and organizations, nor was our rural area ripe for internships and innovative opportunities. As my sister framed it, "We had all this ambition but nowhere to put it."

While the lack of opportunity may have seemed detrimental to our future prospects, I have come to believe it paradoxically had a hidden benefit. At the time, it was incredibly frustrating to exist in an environment so antithetical to our core being. Yet, I have realized that because the opportunities weren't always present, the onus was on us to be bold, proactive, and willing to chart our own course. Looking back, I pinpoint Appalachia's tendency to inhibit future success as crucial to my personal growth. I credit much of my success to what I learned due to the circumstances of growing up in Appalachia.

***

If you recall, following the Parkland shooting, I felt the need to protest for gun reform and hold a school walkout. Seeing as there was no significant force pushing for such action in my area, I took the initiative to organize the efforts.

Similarly, as I became increasingly interested in politics and failed to see any concrete avenues with which I could pursue my interest, I took it upon myself to research opportunities. I ultimately ended up being selected as one of two delegates from Maryland and 104 nationally to attend the prestigious United States Senate Youth Program, where I participated in meetings with the president, cabinet members, senators, ambassadors, intelligence officials, and more. Getting involved in this program involved first being nominated by one's school principal. Schools across the state were sending nominees to compete, but my principal was not aware of the program or its significance. I basically went into his office and nominated myself.

When I traveled to Baltimore to participate in the second round, which consisted of taking a rigorous public affairs exam along with ninety-three others nominated from around Maryland, I was the only one present who lived even remotely close to Western Maryland. I remember arriving at the testing center and walking up to the registration table, only to hear the proctor exclaim, "You're from where?!" It was almost an unwritten rule that Western Maryland would be MIA. It simply would not have been on my radar had I not taken the initiative to go after it myself. The same thing happened when I learned I was one of the top ten test scorers selected to move on to the interview round at the Maryland State Department of Education. They were sort of awestruck I had actually missed school to drive two-and-a-half hours east to downtown Baltimore. In my mind, I was going after an opportunity that was not going to happen otherwise.

After attending the Senate Youth program, I decided to launch a political news podcast with a co-delegate from Iowa. I relentlessly researched and carried out all the podcast and audio production, prepared storylines, contacted guests, and learned how to navigate the world of uploading and publishing podcasts. We ended up producing twelve episodes on every major streaming platform and had the opportunity to interview high-profile guests like Jaime Harrison (former Associate Chair of the Democratic National Committee and current U.S. Senate candidate against Lindsay Graham), Alec

Ross (Secretary of State Hillary Clinton's former Senior Advisor and *New York Times* bestselling author), and J. D. Scholten (US Congressional candidate and hopefully soon-to-be Congressman come November). We did all of this from home while coordinating virtually.

The go-getter mindset and habits cultivated as a byproduct of my upbringing in Appalachia have now translated to me joining numerous clubs and organizations in college, spending a summer doing basketball peace-building work between Catholics and Protestants in Belfast, Northern Ireland, becoming involved in self-designed research on campus, and now writing this book. It manifests in more subtle ways like my comfortability in cold-calling a stranger on LinkedIn who is a higher-up at a company in which I am interested, or my willingness to put myself out there and embrace vulnerability. It's fundamentally a mindset shift, an understanding of not thinking twice about crafting my own path and being unafraid to try and to fail.

In currently attending Bowdoin, I now have a unique vantage point in grappling with my upbringing. Most of my peers and closest friends attended high schools where going to NESCACs or Ivies is the norm, not the exception. Their scholastic upbringings were shaped by hedge fund internships, traveling the world on gap years, and endless opportunities to join slam poetry clubs, improv groups, entrepreneurship initiatives, and more. One could get involved in anything and everything. Sometimes I wonder what it would be like if I lived an alternate life in my friends' shoes. Interested in politics? Well, turns out two of my college friends' closest buddies from home were the campaign managers for a 2020 presidential candidate in the Democratic primary. *They ran a presidential campaign in high school.* Imagine bouncing from study hall straight to an MSNBC interview. That's normal there. Interested in entrepreneurship? Several of my friends had already started companies in high school. "How?" I asked. "Well, that's just what people did" was the reply. Opportunity was for the taking and all you had to do was get involved. Someone else was putting in the leg work.

This is not to discount my friends' achievements. They are incredibly ambitious, creative, and inspiring individuals. That's why they were able to accomplish all they did and continue to do. Yet, in talking to them, even they recognize their nurturing and privileged environment could, and did, lead to a sense of complacency among many of their peers. As one of my friends put it, "At our high school, no matter what, you're going to get into NYU, Boston University, or Northeastern. Put in a little work and you're set for something even better." The sheer amount of opportunities my friends were able to take advantage of was great. Still, they will be the first ones to tell you the same good fortune didn't always breed a sense of bold self-pursuit, persistence, and grit. They were all small fish in a big pond, or perhaps more accurately, moderately-sized fish in a nutrient-dense pond.

I attribute much of my confidence and self-assurance to the parenting I received; however, I'm cognizant that being an outlier in Appalachia also played a large role in lighting a fire under me. It was a blend of the two that has shaped my life trajectory, a blend that could have very easily resulted in a different path. It would have been just as easy to give up along the way, to become totally disillusioned with the surroundings and let the premature "senioritis" build up to an overwhelming degree. I found ways to direct my ambition, but it was difficult not to be overcome with the feeling that all my work was happening in a vacuum, closed off from everything, and yet still necessary to advance and "make it out." Appalachia was not going to propel me forward—I needed to propel myself out.

CHAPTER 7 –

SHOULD I STAY OR SHOULD I GO?

———

As I traverse the rolling hills, a feeling of dread settles into me. The first mountaintop comes into view, lined with endless deciduous green on its gently sloping flanks. Like a photobomber ruining an otherwise holiday-card-worthy family photo, a terraced wasteland of inner-earth and heavy machinery conspicuously stains the mountain's center. A strip mine.

I pass a massive skeleton of exposed rusty steel beams and concrete slats hugging the interstate with an accompanying blue sign exclaiming, *NOAH'S ARK BEING REBUILT HERE!* For over thirty years, the site has supposedly been in the process of being "rebuilt" by a local church. Every time I come home, it remains unchanged—seemingly just like my town.

Making the pilgrimage to rural Western Maryland always manages to take a toll on me. Every time, I try to maintain a positive attitude. Without fail, when I see these landmarks, I'm thrust into a headspace I don't particularly enjoy.

My sister and I have always struggled to identify and articulate exactly what it is about coming home that throws us off. There's an aura about the land, the coal-scarred mountains and incomplete biblical construction projects symbolizing an area stuck in its ways—stagnant, melancholic. It's an overarching feeling that seems to consume us. The transition from the dynamic and vibrant intellectual haven provided by a small liberal arts college sure doesn't help. I remember when my sister would return home from college when I was in high school. She was always excited to see me but deeply affected by returning home. Meanwhile, I, eager to converse with someone from the "outside," peppered her with questions, often to the point of annoyance.

I've always felt out of place in Appalachia. When my senior year classmates talked about "senioritis," I used to half-joke that I've been afflicted since sixth grade. When I now return home from college like my sister once did, the chasm feels ever greater.

Bouncing between the extremes presented by college and home is quite jarring. At college, I am filled with boundless hope. Enveloped in my liberal bubble, stimulating discourse is everywhere. The people are forward-thinking, open-minded, and willing to dive into the minutia of things. Professors are engaging and knowledgeable. Exciting opportunities abound. All of this clashes with the stark reality of life on the outside: designated safe spaces juxtaposed with Confederate flags. Classes devoted to climate change replaced with climate deniers. Racial and economic justice rhetoric becomes inflammatory "America First" talking points. My prior optimism quickly turns into discouragement and cynicism.

Now, this not to say college in general, or Bowdoin specifically, is perfect by any means. As much as I love it, the institution itself can be unreceptive to change and conservative in its own right, entangled by billion-dollar endowments and responsive to the whims of high-profile trustees. And it undoubtedly serves—unintentionally or not—as an assembly line that churns out those armed for a future characterized by the likes of Wall Street, McKinsey & Company, and corporate America at large. On the other end of the spectrum, for all its dynamism, a place like Bowdoin can become bogged down in its own idealism, thus losing its real-world grounding. There can be a tendency to lose sight of the forest for the trees while operating in the vacuum of top-notch academia, resulting in adherence to an interdisciplinarian worldview to such a degree that it can cloud out the bigger picture. The subtleties are certainly important, but when they come at the expense of finding concrete solutions to real-world problems and taking decisive action, they can be distracting. Simply put, an unnecessarily verbose thirty-page journal article steeped in technical academic jargon is admirable; sometimes, however, a one-page press release that clearly distills the main points and is accessible to a broader audience, perhaps even the article's subjects, will do. All that aside, Bowdoin and its peers are incredible places.

My college friends, eager to go home for break after a long semester, are always surprised to hear about my apathy toward doing the same. I haven't been home for more than a few days straight since starting college, save for a few months of remote college in the wake of the coronavirus. "Don't you miss it?" they ask, aghast that I seem unfazed by my infrequent visits. While I look forward to seeing my family, the surrounding environment makes it difficult for me to fully enjoy it. I didn't go home this past winter break, as my mom decided to have a family rendezvous in Maine. I couldn't escape home, however; a friend sent me a Snapchat picture of our local newspaper with the headline: *West Virginia lawmakers vote to let foster care agencies turn away LGBTQ youth, parents.* I logged onto Facebook and was met with a flood of posts opposing Trump's impeachment, one even calling for armed rebellion if he is to be removed. All of a sudden, I am transported back. Feeling a tinge of guilt, I'm happy to be physically removed from all of this.

***

"Do you think you'll ever go back?" I'm often met with this question after telling people about my experiences in Appalachia. Each time, I hesitate, trying to find the right words to communicate my conflicting feelings. I think back to the spiel I've heard a million times from people in my small town: "You might want to leave now, but you'll miss it eventually. You'll want to come back and raise a family here."

I have a hard time believing I'll ever have a complete 180 like this. I don't know exactly where my future lies, but I know my tribe isn't at home. The differences feel irreconcilable. Its culturally and economically regressive nature—a lethal combination of suffocating social views and scarce economic opportunity—has permanently propelled me outward.

But I then wonder if my thought patterns are part of the problem. Don't I have a moral responsibility to return home, to do my best to ameliorate its issues—not as a savior, but as a concerned citizen well-aware of the region's pressing challenges? To do otherwise would make me complicit in its downfall, no? By attaching myself to the glimmer of hope provided by places far from Appalachia, aren't I just further perpetuating the "brain drain" that contributes to the region's economic woes?

This internal debate often rages in my head when I'm enjoying the luxuries of not being home. When I'm reaping the rewards of a top-notch college education—networking, exposure to the institutions and powerful special interests that shape our country, being thrust into a place of relative privilege among ever higher echelons of society—I'm continually in a process of being further removed from Appalachia. It's Goldman Sachs dropping by campus to recruit, classmates from "just outside Boston," and billion-dollar endowments. It's Rhodes Scholarships and gap years, legacies in college admissions and ski trips to Vail. Regardless of whether I actively buy into each of these things, their mere presence in my life serves to siphon me off, to divert me away from my roots. It's not just how I feel about home that matters anymore.

I compare where I am to Appalachia and I feel guilty. I know I shouldn't. It's not that my current place and future path come at the expense of those at home, but there is something about looking back at home from the outside that troubles me at some level.

Last year, I spoke to Alec Ross, a West Virginia native who went on to be a tech entrepreneur, *New York Times* bestselling author, and former senior official in the Obama Administration. I asked him how he balanced this tension—rising from Appalachian origins to work at the highest levels of government and private sector—and his thoughts about potentially returning to the region. He expressed similar reservations about going home, saying, "It's too backward-looking economically. Culturally, it's too regressive. Those of us who have kids tend to want to raise our kids in an environment that embraces openness. It would be difficult for me to take my kids in Maryland and put them in public school in West Virginia, where I know that many of the views that they're going to hear are going to be variants of what comes out of the mouth of Donald Trump."

He continued, "[Appalachia] propels people out but then what may be worse, it then keeps them out. I love the region. The tension is wanting its people to do well, but profound disappointment with its leadership and the political choices made by its citizens."

I've thought about Alec's comments a lot. I want to *want* to go home. When I see college friends eager to visit friends and places from home, I find myself nostalgic for something I've never experienced, like seeing old black and white photographs depicting people's lives in an era much before my time.

I know I still care about home. I would like to work on problems afflicting the region in some capacity, and I recognize I don't have to physically plant myself in the troughs to do so. Yet, for all my yearning for a non-existent relationship with my hometown, I'll never really fit in there. The complicating part is I'm appreciative of this fact. For me, the tension lies in wishing I wasn't an outlier, while simultaneously being incredibly grateful I was. Grateful to have grown up in a family that stood opposite to much of the rhetoric I heard growing up among my close-minded peers. Grateful to have not been swept up in a stifling small-town worldview that quashes big ambitions. Grateful to be able to look beyond our little blip on the map and recognize there is a big wide world out there.

I'm still left with profound disappointment. Yet, I'm also filled with immense gratitude.

CHAPTER 8 –

POLITICAL REALITIES

———

When I see maps depicting the liberal coasts' blue standing in stark contrast to the heartland's red, I always look closely at the panhandle of Western Maryland, thinking to myself, "Hey, they missed a couple of liberals in there. Not many, but we exist!" I imagine my family as a tiny blue dot, otherwise imperceptible in the pool of red.

When I used to watch Stephen Colbert or read a progressive outlet online, I would chuckle to myself, speculating there was a very real chance I was the only such web traffic in my entire county. Is such a possibility really that far off?

Somewhere, somehow, I felt like a National Security Agency (NSA) officer would be combing through surveillance, suddenly getting an alert that raises a (quite literal) red flag: "Web traffic to *Jacobin Magazine* reported. Location: Western Maryland." *Hmm, that seems odd,* the hypothetical intelligence official thinks to himself.

Yet, for how unusual it was for my family to exist as a liberal bastion in Appalachia, I've come to realize that ironically, perhaps the single most determinative factor in shaping my political appetite has been the place itself. Of course, it goes without mentioning that the seeds were first planted by familial influence and other associated socialization factors.

For instance, for a number of years growing up, we attended Sunday fellowship at the Unitarian Universalist (UU) church—or as I describe it when asked by someone unfamiliar with UU: "liberal, hippie, nature shit." It's like if Jerry Falwell actually just decided he was Henry David Thoreau and declared that the trees and seasons reigned supreme. How could I ever emerge from years of being classically conditioned to derive legitimacy from Mother Nature and science, only to turn around and cast a vote for Ted Cruz? Seems impossible!

Then there was the cyclical nature of National Public Radio radio's influence in my life, eating breakfast to the tune of Steve Inskeep's *Morning Edition* and returning home from school, only to follow the distinctive tenor of Robert Siegel to the kitchen where my mother would be cooking dinner whilst being serenaded by *All Things Considered*.

Or, there's the fact that immediately upon entering my home, you are confronted with two giant tapestries: one of the Buddha and one that exhibits the Grateful Dead's lyric, "You Are The Eyes Of The World," complete with two massive blue eyes staring down from the wall above. It's almost like those eyes silently followed me during my upbringing, gently steering me toward the Whole Foods and Birkenstocks of the world and away from the dominant ideologies of my peers. I mean really, who the hell has Buddha and Jerry Garcia prominently displayed upon entering the door… in *APPALA-CHIA*? It's safe to say the electoral map did not catch that one.

When you look at it from this perspective—considering the peripheral influences of UU, NPR, Jerry Garcia, and much more—it seems all but certain I would grow up seeing the world a certain way. What seems less certain, however, is the extent to which those beliefs endured despite the surrounding environment in which I grew up. People are often surprised to hear the asymmetry between my progressive values and my Appalachian upbringing, perhaps thinking I would be conservative given its influence in the region. However, when I look back, I see that not only did I retain my worldview but that it was actually largely bred by the place itself. Appalachia, more than anything else, served to further solidify and entrench my political leanings.

We often think of echo chambers as a root cause of polarization. After all, we get our news from different places, curate our social media follows accordingly, and even physically sort ourselves into different geographical locations. In the wake of the World Wide Web's rise in the '90s, MIT researchers Marshall Van Alstyne and Erik Brynjolfsson warned of the dangers of our digitally interconnected world, saying:

> "Individuals empowered to screen out material that does not conform to their existing preferences may form virtual cliques, insulate themselves from opposing points of view, and reinforce their biases... Internet users can seek out interactions with like-minded individuals who have similar values, and thus become less likely to trust important decisions to people whose values differ from their own."[23]

Paradoxically, I think being exposed to points of view that contradicted my own—exposure the researchers cite as

---

23   Marshall Van Alstyne and Erik Brynjolfsson, "Global Village or Cyber-Balkans? Modeling and Measuring the Integration of Electronic Communities," *Management Science* 51, No. 6 (June 2005): 865-866.

important to counteracting polarization—actually left me more steadfast in my own convictions. Simply put, being surrounded by so much conservatism, especially social conservatism, pushed me further left.

It was the talk of "Mexicans taking our jobs," "Women should not be President," and racial slurs I would rather not say. It was being peppered with climate change skepticism by the attendant filling up the tank at the local gas station. It was the Facebook rants about welfare queens and socialists taking our guns, and pushback to Michelle Obama's attempts to "make us eat healthy" with her nutritional school lunch initiatives while simultaneously taking away our God-given right to eat crap if we please… *Thanks, Obama*. What's next, full-blown communism?

That one was a big one. No tribulation was too big or too small to warrant a "Thanks, Obama." Fresh carrots now an option for school lunch? Thanks, Obama. Wasn't granted a snow day for school? Thanks, Obama. Coal experiencing a decline in the region? Thanks, Obama. Everything seemed to find its way back to the Obamas, regardless of how little their influence was really felt in our day-to-day lives.

Living in Appalachia meant I didn't need to turn on Fox News to break out of an echo chamber. I simply needed to hop aboard my public school bus. I was physically confronted with it on a day-to-day basis, and as much as I tried to keep an open mind, many of the things I heard struck me as plain wrong. That being said, it's important to note that not everybody expressed these viewpoints, although they were far more frequent than I would like to think.

This exposure also spurred another interest of mine: political satire. My love for political satire was born out of my existence in an environment that introduced me to all sorts of far-right talking points. To deal with the absurdity of it all, folks like Jon Stewart and Stephen Colbert became coping mechanisms of sorts—people who provided an outlet by satirizing many of the sentiments I grew up hearing. I think back to Obama's final White House Correspondents' Dinner in 2016. You may remember Obama's use of Keegan-Michael Key as his "anger translator"—i.e. someone who could provide unfiltered elaboration on Obama's otherwise polished, politically correct statements. As Obama says in his speech, "Despite our differences, we can count on the press to shed light on the most important issues of the day." Key immediately clarifies, "And we can count on Fox News to terrify old white people with some nonsense! Sharia Law is coming to Cleveland—run for the damn hills!" I remember watching this live, reflecting on how many times I witnessed peers repeat similar fearmongering. Key's riff, although brief, provided some solace.[24]

I came to appreciate political satire for its ability to cut through the noise, especially in the Trump era. In a time in which traditional news media struggles to effectively cover Trump and his spin doctors, I admire the ability to move beyond the talking points and panel debates—and instead encourage audiences to think critically by making light of the absurd. My own humor and personality, in general (much of it derived from the experiences and interactions of my upbringing) were coping mechanisms. More and more, I think satire became a way of dealing with the trials and tribulations of life at home, frustrations that often manifested themselves in jokes and political impressions.

---

24 "2015 White House Correspondents' Dinner," *C-SPAN*, 1:36:02, April 25, 2015.

Our living room was my first stage. There was a sort of unspoken tradition in our household. Some evenings, when my sister and I had returned from after-school sports practice and my mom and dad had returned home from their respective duties, we would gather in the living room: them on the couch, my sister and I sharing the spotlight before them. We would take turns, reenacting the most ridiculous scenes from our day: the kid on the bus who had muttered the thing about the Muslims, the teacher who had expressed bewilderment upon hearing about Vermont's status as a state, the local newspaper story about the police chase of ATV vehicles darting around town.

Satire was the only way to accept and make sense of our reality, and to keep going. To an extent, dad had the luxury of being immersed in an academic bubble and mom had her "wild women" crew, but my sister and I were in public school, confronting the realities of home head-on.

This was how we dealt with it all—by reclaiming power over the offensive and absurd things we encountered on any given day.

My parents, for their part, would not really say anything in response to our living room shenanigans. They laughed, maybe shook their heads, but generally remained observers. I think this ultimately speaks to a larger trend about their impact on our perceptions of home and politics. They were, of course, highly influential in our lives and in shaping our worldviews, but we listened to what we heard at home, school, and throughout our travels, consolidated our experiences, and made our own decisions. Our viewpoints were formulated on our own volition, amidst the backdrop of life under informative parents and an equally illuminating surrounding region.

While my politics were largely informed by my aversion to the talking points expressed by those with whom I grew up, another major factor was living in a region that desperately needed the government assistance it so condemned. In my town, "liberal" was a dirty word, a political pejorative reserved for those who were in favor of government tyranny. This was ironic, of course, given that government programs were of great benefit to many of the area's residents.

Growing up in a community touched by poverty, few jobs, and a declining tax base demonstrated to me the necessity of government assistance. I witnessed the impact of federal programs like the ARC in stemming the region's nosedive. I saw the need for investment in the region and the importance of a social safety net to get people on their feet and transition in the midst of what Andrew Yang calls the "4th Industrial Revolution." As he warns, we are undergoing the greatest economic transformation in our history, one that entails job losses totaling tens of millions due to automation. Blue-collar jobs like manufacturing, retail, and truck driving will essentially become obsolete, further exacerbating an area that has already witnessed coal's downfall and the lack of any suitable replacement.

We often hear the left's responses to some of these issues: things like Medicare for All, free public college, clean energy investments, and a $15 minimum wage. These lofty proposals can sometimes feel like distant, idealistic visions, or merely applause lines in a candidate's speech. My surroundings, however, helped me connect them to the real world. These weren't just abstract ideas but tangible efforts that could make a difference in my community. I guess oddly enough, my conservative environment had a way of grounding the most progressive ideals; I saw the place that needed them the most turned out to be the least receptive.

This fact was and still is a tough thing to swallow. It leaves me cynical yet determined to change some of the things I witnessed growing up. My time in Appalachia has spurred my interest in politics as an avenue to remedy some of these issues and has shaped my political ideology immeasurably. Living in the region meant I now feel attuned to a host of issues of which I otherwise would be unaware. It has given me a holistic and well-rounded perspective of which I feel fortunate to have received. I am grateful for the place that has challenged me, all the while facilitating my understanding of the world.

PART 4:

MOVING FORWARD

CHAPTER 9 –

COAL

I held up my phone and listened intently to the YouTube video: "76,000 coal workers is less than you'd expect. Although in the areas where they are concentrated, coal mines are central to the community. Some schools have miners as mascots for their sports teams...."[25]

In the graphics box beside the anchor's head appeared a burly coal miner, complete with a yellow headlamp and a menacing grimace. The name *Mountain Ridge Miners* popped up in bold print.

It was at this moment I dropped my phone off the side of my bed, my mouth agape. My high school mascot being satirized on a nationally televised show that regularly captures an audience of close to 20 million people? Quite literally our 15 seconds of fame. *What?!*

I had been catching up on John Oliver's satirical investigative journalism show *Last Week Tonight*. This particular week's episode centered on the role of coal in America, a topic that piqued my interest given its importance in my

---

25 LastWeekTonight, "Coal: Last Week Tonight with John Oliver (HBO)," *YouTube*, 24:20, Jun. 17, 2017.

area. I've always appreciated Oliver's willingness to dive into obscure and under-reported topics—subjects like nuclear waste, felony disenfranchisement, and net neutrality. Yet, even I didn't expect him to shed light on coal country, let alone point out the peculiarity of my high school mascot. It's almost quite fitting that the one time my region seems to break through and reach—albeit brief—national prominence, the topic talked about in jest is the one thing on which the area prides itself: coal.

I have to laugh when I think back on this moment. I've always thought a coal miner is a strange mascot, but I guess I had become desensitized to it at a certain point. Coal is synonymous with Appalachia (especially my town), so it was a somewhat obvious choice to represent my school. However, being reminded of it in a satirical format reinforced its oddity for me. I like to joke it was at that moment I knew I needed to leave Appalachia. Our school fan section at sporting events was led by a student fully in costume as a coal miner: cloaked in fake soot, wielding a pickax, donning a headlamp. The whole nine yards. What happened to Eagles, Knights, or Bulldogs?

[Side note: My middle school was the Mt. Savage Indians, named after a local surveyor named Thomas Savage. Places are named after people all the time, but no one thought "savage" would be a problematic modifier before Indians? Mt. Savage Lions, Falcons, Lightning, or really anything else under the sun would have been just fine! My current college mascot? Polar Bears. So, in sequential order… "Savage" Indians, Coal Miners, and Polar Bears—name a more eclectic mascot experience.]

Satire aside, John Oliver was right. Although coal is a rapidly dwindling profession, it still plays an important role in my community. Coal is integral to the region's heritage and identity. It's more than a raw material or profession. It's a glorified way of life. People are proud of what the coal miner represents: grit, working-class ethos, nostalgia for times gone past.

It doesn't matter that coal is a dying industry or nationwide, more people actually work at Carl Jr.'s franchises than in the mines.[26] Our local museum still prominently displays replicas of working coal mines and dusty relics from bygone times. My high school teachers proudly explained that coal from our area is said to have been key to twentieth-century wartime success. Remembering coal's history in these ways is not inherently a problem. I understand the pride and think in many cases, it's warranted. When it serves to cloud out the bigger picture, however, a new pattern emerges.

***

Coal is not coming back. You wouldn't know it if you took a drive on the local country roads littered with *Obama Kills Coal* signs. It's as if coal is just temporarily out of commission, not on a century-long decline. It is framed as a commodity momentarily being squandered upon, waiting for a successor to revive it.

Donald Trump presented himself as that successor, promising to bring back coal jobs by slashing environmental regulations, despite the fact that doing so would have—and has—had marginal effects on job growth. Wearing a hard hat, he feigned interest at a 2016 Charleston, West Virginia

---

26 Derek Thompson, "The White House Exaggerated the Growth of Coal Jobs by About 5,000 Percent," *The Atlantic*, June 6, 2017.

rally, pumping his fists and making fake mining motions as the crowd cheered:

> "We love clean, beautiful West Virginia coal. We love it. And you know that's indestructible stuff. In times of war, in times of conflict, you can blow up those windmills. They fall down real quick. You can blow up those pipelines. They go like this and you're not going to fix them too fast. You can do a lot of things to those solar panels. But you know what you can't hurt? Coal… We are back. The coal industry is back."[27]

Of course, this was patently false; coal is not back, and many in the crowd had felt the economic impacts of its absence firsthand. Still, his campaign promises were welcomed with open arms throughout the region. West Virginians went to the ballot boxes to send him into office with his second-largest statewide margin of victory behind Wyoming.

Paradoxically, it goes without mentioning that the GOP platform of gutting Obamacare and social services would be disastrous to a region heavily dependent on welfare. Not only does West Virginia, as an elderly and unhealthy state, disproportionately rely on programs such as Medicare, but nearly 20 percent of West Virginia's workers are also themselves employed in health services.[28] Weakening the Affordable Care Act would certainly yield more job losses in the healthcare sector than any potential gains to coal.

---

27 Linda Qui and John Schwartz, "Trump's False Claims About Coal, the Environment and West Virginia," *The New York Times*, Aug. 21, 2018.

28 Paul Krugman, "Coal Country Is a State of Mind", *The New York Times*, March 31, 2017.

This makes Appalachia's dedication to Trump and the GOP even more puzzling. A region entirely voting against its own interests. Why?

As *New York Times* columnist Paul Krugman puts it, "'Coal country' residents weren't voting to preserve what they have, or had, until recently; they were voting on behalf of a story their region tells about itself, a story that hasn't been true for a generation or more. Their Trump votes weren't even about the region's interests; they were about cultural symbolism."[29]

My high school mascot is that cultural symbolism in action. The school opened just over ten years ago, replacing one that had been a mainstay in the region for over 100 years. It was a chance to usher in a new era, to tell a new story. Instead, it reached back into a bygone time, re-instating the coal miner back upon his throne.

I understand there is perhaps a piece to coal mining culture in my community I'll never truly understand due to my family's absent Appalachian background. I can respect coal's historical importance. I can admire the miners who have battled black lung and automation and the global forces that have chipped away at their livelihood of chipping away. Coal quite literally powered the Industrial Revolution. America, in part, owes its nascent superpower rise to industrious individuals deep inside the earth in a little town in rural Western Maryland. I can recognize all of this.

And yet, for all my appreciation, I didn't have ancestors who worked in the mines or depended on it to live. My family did not see coal ebb and flow, watch new sources of energy enter the market, or experience the drawn-out fall

<hr>

29 Ibid.

of a profession, a lifestyle, a story. Maybe this missing piece explains why I just can't fathom the political behaviors of a region. Maybe it explains how, despite the fact my parents were hard-working middle-class Americans who likewise appreciated coal's impact, my family was somehow perceived as not quite Appalachian.

The ethos was off and you just had to have been there to "get it," I guess.

I have a hard time accepting this dynamic, however; the unspoken labeling of us as outsiders peering in. Coal had its day and now it's time to adapt, to let go of a narrative that becomes less true as each day passes. We can honor its legacy, while not letting it impede progress. We can simultaneously hold in our minds these two supposedly conflicting truths.

As our planet burns, we can identify coal as the root of the problem, while supporting those who mine it. These are the parents and grandparents and great-grandparents of people with whom I grew up going to school; folks who simply endeavored to put food on the table. Taking action on climate change does not mean demonizing or abandoning them, but rather, assisting them through a tumultuous transition—one that is far more than a job change but both a personal and cultural shift. This means job retraining for the few still employed in the mines and broader investment in a region reeling from the loss of secondary and tertiary economic activities made possible by coal in its heyday. Coal may be in the rearview mirror, but it remains to be seen whether mascots will be the only thing to take its place.

CHAPTER 10 –

CONSERVATISM

———

"When you're voting for a guy [named] Donald Trump who inherited $200 million when he was twenty-one years old and is from New York City… like, you're out of mind if you think he cares about you, just because he comes and puts a hard hat on and says we're gonna get coal going again."

I had been talking to Alec Ross about the GOP's stronghold over the region. "West Virginia—if you just look at it economically, it should be one of the most progressive places in the country, and instead, it's one of the most politically conservative," he lamented.

He spoke to a trend that has frustrated me for as long as I can remember. Why is Appalachia beholden to conservatism when it is precisely such an ideology that perpetuates the region's woes?

I remember when we had a mock school vote in 2016 ahead of the presidential election. Trump won and Hillary got *destroyed*. Fringe candidate Gary Johnson even had higher approval—and I know for a fact that few people in my school even knew who he was. I sat there in my homeroom overhearing the results broadcasted on the PA system, unsurprised at the results, yet still in a sort of disbelief.

Appalachia is conservative—*really* conservative. But Alec's right, it just doesn't add up. The region has the most to gain by embracing progressive populist economics and much to lose by abandoning the public institutions that keep it afloat—things like the Appalachian Regional Commission, the university in my town, a social safety net.

I get it—politics can be confusing, intimidating, and frustrating. It's easy to become cynical and reject the system entirely. I mean, what has DC done for me lately? Politicians can seem aloof and out of touch with the concerns of the everyday people, and many of our most pressing political issues are incredibly complex.

Voting in Appalachia's best interest, however, is not. One party explicitly ran on denying coverage for pre-existing conditions, rolling back the Affordable Care Act, and kicking people off their healthcare. One party did not. One party has historically rallied around strengthening labor protections, bolstering unions, and sticking up for the middle-class. The other recently passed a 1.5 trillion-dollar tax cut for the wealthy, the benefits of which have, unsurprisingly, not trickled down to the middle-class.[30] One party wants to expand Social Security, Medicare, and other vital social service benefits. The other prides itself on gutting these programs.

By no means do I agree with everything the Democratic Party stands for. In fact, I still think the party leadership is oftentimes too centrist, too content with the status quo, too willing to cater to special interests and corporate elites at the expense of the working class. Nonetheless, by and large, the party is far more attuned to the concerns of working

---

30   Galen Hendriks, Seth Hanlon, and Michael Madowitz, "Trump's Corporate Tax Cut Is Not Trickling Down," *Center for American Progress*, Sept. 26, 2019.

people than the GOP, a trend made patently obvious in its policy platforms and reflected in modern era voting coalitions. The distinctions between the parties are quite clear and easy to distinguish.

These distinctions are especially important when it comes to Appalachia. Healthcare matters more than ever in a region that often finds itself on the wrong end of lists detailing America's health disparities. Economic inequality matters in a place where mobility is hard to come by and poverty runs rampant. Labor protections matter for trade workers and manufacturers and yes, coal miners. Appalachians are among the nation's greatest beneficiaries of progressive policy.

This is why I can't fathom the dislike for the Democratic Party and the blatant voting against economic self-interest. I understand each person has the right to form his/her own beliefs, and every individual's decision-making process entails different considerations, many of which are personal. Yet, the elephant in the room is that for the most part, Appalachians consistently vote to perpetuate the cycle by disregarding the facts!

There are some obvious explanations for this. Namely, conservatives have won over on social issues—appealing to divisive topics that play well in the region, like guns and abortion. Even more importantly, conservative operatives are incredibly adept at exploiting human psychology for their own ends. When I spoke to Alec, he spoke of palingenesis: i.e. the weaponization of a utopian past that may or may not have existed for political gain. As he puts it, "Right-wing populists tend to do a much better job than progressives in utilizing palingenesis. You know when they say 'Make America Great Again,' they're hearkening back to a time in the 1950s when... people had union jobs. At 6:00... Dad would sit at the head of a table where mom had cooked dinner, and you know 6:30, they watched the news on TV, and at 7:30, Dad was bowling. That past is not as neat as its caricature, but the mythology is powerful and the populist right has historically done a very good job at that."

It's the same sort of psychological appeal used throughout history by fascists attempting to orient the country toward a "rebirth." It's a unifying principle, a rallying cry used to stir up our most primitive desires and concoct a story from which the hive mentality emerges. We want to join together for *something*.

It's just like the narrative Appalachia tells itself about coal, a narrative that reaches back into the days in which Appalachia (supposedly) reigned supreme. The idea behind "Make America Great Again"—much like the infamous Southern Strategy conservatives have relied upon since the 1960s—channels pent-up resentment with the current state of affairs and longing for the past, regardless of its accuracy. Some of it is just innocuous yearning for the good ole days, whatever that may entail. It is worth pointing out, however, that much of it is wrapped up in racism and xenophobia and a return to patriarchal society. Either way, it's effective.

The other thing conservatives have done very well is divide us—make it us vs. them. As Alec puts it, "It's not your fault that these jobs left. It's the Mexicans' fault. It's not your fault that your culture appears to be crumbling. It's the fault of a Muslim Kenyan president. This whole idea of shifting responsibility from the self to someone on the outside, from an internal locus of control to an external locus of control, is really powerful."

Progressives—especially those who are college-educated—meanwhile, want to talk about what we can do better. They want to dive into the minutia of things, explore the nuance, discuss the complex, interdisciplinary factors behind the issues we face. This is all great in theory. In fact, it's one of the reasons why I love the liberal arts college experience. It's crucial, however, to recognize that an elite private liberal arts institution is not representative of America. While I think it's important to care about the nitty-gritty, it's even more important to recognize most people simply *don't*.

A steelworker doesn't want to hear he lost his job because high-powered lawyers helped the company outsource overseas by exploiting tax loopholes, or because automation and machine learning technologies have rendered the job obsolete, or because of any number of other reasons that aren't as clean-cut as us vs. them, victim and abuser. He wants to be able to blame immigrants, or socialism, or political correctness, or any other buzzword the right has effectively weaponized—things they have primed us to automatically loathe and blame for our problems.

This binary system is obviously incredibly problematic. It breeds polarization and tribalism, bringing out the worst in our politics. But once again, conservatives have tapped into the American psyche, relying on dog-whistle politics to prey on our most primal impulses. Problematic? Yes. Smart? At a certain point, you have to give them credit.

Here is where I think some of the burden falls on progressives, namely those who are highly educated. We can keep the nuance, pride ourselves on the fine-details, and unveil comprehensive policies to tackle pressing issues; yet, we have to package it better. We need to boil things down and explain them in black and white terms. We need to use everyday words used by everyday people and not write speeches that require a dictionary, a thesaurus, an encyclopedia, a PhD, a resident policy wonk, and a refreshed Twitter feed all on hand to understand.

Republicans quite simply do not care about being caught red-handed with inflammatory rhetoric or thinly veiled attempts to provoke fear and anxiety toward the "other." They actively try to muddy the waters—propagating conspiracy theories about Uranium One, George Soros, the Deep State, and too many others to count, sowing distrust in the American electoral system, and eagerly coming to Trump's aid despite his constant mendacious behavior. And they have no shame about pandering to Appalachia's voters, while screwing them over in plain sight with giveaways to insulated elites.

Through all of this, they accrue power. Even more importantly, they fundamentally understand that power begets power. Winning elections allows the opportunity to tighten rules on subsequent elections. Installing justices on the Supreme Court provides a generational fail-safe if Democrats cry foul on their actions. They realize that politics is a game, and they are hitting jump shots while Democrats are still pleading with the refs.

I am not condoning these methods. Rather, I hope Democrats likewise start playing their own sort of hardball. We need to challenge conservatives at their own game and stop playing checkers when they're playing chess. We are too insistent on taking the high road. Although well-intentioned, it just ends up hurting the very people we want to help. It hurts the people in the communities I grew up with when we allow GOP candidates to knowingly deceive voters, revert to tribalistic appeals, and enact policies that advance personal political interests at the expense of constituent welfare. It also hurts the people in the communities I grew up with when we over-complicate everything with academic rhetoric and abstract ideals, thus opening the door for Republicans.

I don't know what the exact right approach is, but from my experience existing in environments on opposite ends of the political and socioeconomic spectrum, a few things have become evident. The type of liberal that exists in my anthropology class is not the type of voter we need to court. We've already won them over. It's the person struggling to transition in a rapidly changing economy, the laid-off mill worker trying to put food on the table, the retiree struggling to keep up with medical bills. It's the kind of people in my area who have seen their community hollow out. The folks who aren't beholden to a party just for partisanship's sake, but who want to see who is speaking to the issues they care about, who will revive an area in decline. We need to remind people of the good ole days—the days of the unions that built this country, strong Social Security benefits and pensions, the possibility of living a decent life. In this way, we can harness nostalgia as a tool for progress.

Perhaps we shouldn't abandon progressive populist rhetoric but further lean into it. If we want to compete, we have to speak to the issues working people care about; things like healthcare, education, income inequality, and wage growth. We have to counter the image of us as out-of-touch liberals (no matter how flawed that portrayal is) by tailoring our message to everyday folks. It will be an uphill battle. The right-wing media apparatus is deeply entrenched in the culture. I remember Fox News being the default show in restaurants and doctor's office waiting rooms, the Rush Limbaugh rants so commonplace on the radio. We will have to overcome the onslaught of talking heads depicting us as the enemy.

But there are a few things that make me hopeful. There's a reason Bernie found success in the Rust Belt and had a somewhat surprising level of Bernie-Trump crossover support in 2016. They both spoke to pent-up anxieties and grievances, fulfilling populist desires that manifested themselves in support for two radically different candidates. Meanwhile, although not entirely justified given her record, Hillary was often negatively viewed as one who would perpetuate the status quo. It's clear people are angry, fearful, and hungry for change. It seems to me we have an opportunity to divert these feelings for positive ends.

Maybe I'm being naive or overly optimistic, but I see an opportunity to change course, to reverse conservatism's chokehold on my area. A chance to challenge who has the authority to tell Appalachia's story.

EPILOGUE

—

The ideal of going to school in a dynamic, forward-thinking environment was the light at the end of the tunnel when I sat in class next to MAGA hats and Confederate flag sweatshirts. I could not wait for the pendulum to swing the other direction, to be surrounded by those who largely shared my values. Now that I'm here, I feel as though I have had a chance to blossom after missing out on such a dynamic for most of my life. There's a tension, though, as I'm pulled farther and farther away from the environment in which I grew up. Don't get me wrong, the liberal bubble is great. After years living among a tribe with whom I felt little allegiance, I have embraced the bubble with open arms. In the short term, it's a reprieve, a chance to be surrounded by the people I wish I met much earlier and to have the conversations for which I long yearned. But I am likewise the first one to know that it's also a chance to become removed, to forget about day-to-day life in the mountains of Western Maryland, to be blinded to the people and issues right in my backyard. The liberal bubble is great, but it is, after all, a bubble, just like the bubble presented by home.

By the same token, it has given me an opportunity to reflect meaningfully on my past and re-focus my vision to not lose sight of my roots. As I progress through this experience, I do so with a critical eye. I now find myself among the same people folks back home resented for being out-of-touch. I'm constantly reminded of the place I grew up, the way its inhabitants perceived so-called bastions of elitism and liberal politics, and my place in all of this.

Growing up in Appalachia was often very trying for me. However, I now feel deep gratitude for the places and perspectives to which I was exposed during my upbringing. Western Maryland is a beautiful region of the country, and I feel fortunate to have had the opportunity to hike, bike, and generally be immersed in it. Living there was an education that extended far beyond the classroom walls—a grounding many of the people with whom I'm currently surrounded did not receive. I learned how to conduct myself in a hostile arena, channel my frustrations to productive ends, and walk the tightrope of knowing when to express myself and, perhaps more importantly, when to exercise restraint and listen. I adopted the long view and didn't allow the situation at hand to consume me. I found ways to make light of the situation with grit and empathy and yes, a heavy dose of sarcasm. I became a more perceptive and curious individual by nature of being immersed in a perplexing place. And I became okay with the idea of operating independently and tackling things on my own. I cultivated the ability to converse with people from all levels of the socioeconomic and ideological spectrum—people I am not sure I would have otherwise encountered to the same extent had I not grown up where I did. Whether it was the guy pumping gas lecturing me on the hoax of climate change or now the industry bigwigs dropping by Bowdoin to lecture me on big data or macroeconomic policy, I feel comfortable code-switching between two ends of the human experience. I pride myself on being able to find at least *one* thing in common to carry on a conversation with whomever I encounter. This is one skill in particular whose value and rarity has become ever-more apparent from my current vantage point at Bowdoin.

I'm reminded of a story my sister once told me: the time several of her fellow Middlebury students traveled to rural Appalachia on a school-sponsored alternative spring break program for what was officially marketed as "intercultural communication." White America meets white America—and yet, the two segments of society are so foreign, so incompatible, it warrants a spring break community service trip. How odd it must have been for my sister to see her peers visit her home, viewing it wide-eyed like some sort of enigma? Privilege can be blinding.

***

I often think of the time my mom uncovered a bombshell discovery in a family history book written by her grandmother's cousin. In an ironic turn of events, my great-great-grandparents emigrated from Scotland in 1865, passing through Ellis Island, and ultimately landing nowhere else than Lonaconing, Maryland—a mere nine miles from where I sit writing this book right now. Out of all the places in the world, they landed here to put down roots in the New World! And to think it was their first stop, no less. Not only am I Appalachian, but I am also... an OG Appalachian? Not to mention that Lonaconing, or "Coney," is about as "down the crick" as it gets. *What?*

My mom was speechless when she found out. I think I was in fourth or fifth grade at the time. She just could not fathom that we had ancestry in the region, let alone ancestry that could claim to have been here before many of the families that were the "true locals." My parents were not armed with this knowledge when they moved here. We were, after all, always the outsiders who thought we had no heritage in the area. Granted, my ancestors soon moved out of the region, pushing northward as new generations came into being. Otherwise, we surely would have known about their presence.

In looking back, my mom recalls a pent-up grievance in light of this new information. It was an "I told you so" moment. She remembers feeling like a spectator during her time on city council, peering in on the "insiders" who could lay claim to the region and its family tree. The mayor never seemed to give her the time of day for a number of reasons—namely, she possessed the lethal combination of not having a Y chromosome *and* holding progressive views. Undergirding all of this, however, was the simple fact that we were not from here. She lacked the legitimacy of a true inhabitant of the region.

Now that the myth of our origins has been shattered, what now? What if the alternate history had transpired and we belonged by default? What if it was more widely known we were here, earlier even, than most? I frequently find myself coming back to these hypotheticals. All of a sudden, I am consumed with a rush of thoughts. I think about how much easier everything would have been and how much more comfortable I would have felt and what a different experience I would have had. It's tempting to long for that version of history. And then I pause for a second and am immediately overcome with the conclusion I ultimately land upon: for all the resentment I harbor for the region and all the frustrations I endured, I would not have had the experience any other way. I'm grateful to have grown up here, to have been an outlier, and to have been perceived as such.

My identity has been fundamentally shaped by the first chapter of my life spent in Appalachia; no matter where I end up, or who I associate with, it is a piece of me. A piece that carries conflicting feelings of frustration and gratitude, confusion and appreciation. A piece that feels close, yet deeply unfamiliar. A piece I still struggle to fully understand, and yet a piece, nonetheless.

APPENDIX

Introduction

Bishop, Bill. *The Big Sort: Why the Clustering of Like-Minded America Is Tearing Us Apart.* Boston: Houghton Mifflin, 2008.

"Partisanship and Political Animosity in 2016." *Pew Research Center.* June 22, 2016. https://www.people-press.org/2016/06/22/partisanship-and-political-animosity-in-2016/.

Chapter 1

"County Economic Status and Distressed Areas in Appalachia." *Appalachian Regional Commission.* https://www.arc.gov/appalachian_region/CountyEconomicStatusandDistressedAreasinAppalachia.asp.

"County Economic Status, Fiscal Year 2020: Appalachian Maryland." *Appalachian Regional Commission.* https://www.arc.gov/reports/region_report.asp?FIPS=24999&REPORT_ID=76.

"County Economic Status in Appalachia, FY 2020." *Appalachian Regional Commission.* https://www.arc.gov/research/MapsofAppalachia.asp?MAP_ID=149.

"Education—High School and College Completion Rates, 2013-2017: Appalachian Maryland." *Appalachian Regional Commission.* https://www.arc.gov/reports/region_report.asp?FIPS=24999&REPORT_ID=79.

"Interactive Data." *Creating a Culture of Health in Appalachia: Disparities and Bright Spots.* https://healthinappalachia.org/disparities-report/interactive-report/.

Rodricks, Dan. "Hefty price tag for Western Maryland succession." *The Baltimore Sun.* September 14, 2013. https://www.baltimoresun.com/maryland/bs-xpm-2013-09-14-bs-md-rodricks-0915-20130914-story.html.

Stebbins, Samuel. "These are the poorest cities in every state in the US." *USA TODAY.* May 7, 2019. https://www.usatoday.com/picture-gallery/money/2019/05/01/poorest-town-in-every-state/39431927/.

"The Appalachian Region." *Appalachian Regional Commission.* https://www.arc.gov/appalachian_region/TheAppalachian-Region.asp.

"2018 Crime in the United States: Maryland." *FBI: UCR.* https://ucr.fbi.gov/crime-in-the-u.s/2018/crime-in-the-u.s.-2018/tables/table-8/table-8-state-cuts/maryland.xls.

"Unintentional Drug- and Alcohol-Related Intoxication Deaths in
Maryland, 2018." *Maryland Department of Health.* May 2019.
https://bha.health.maryland.gov/Documents/Annual_2018_
Drug_Intox_Report.pdf.

Wallace, David Foster. "Transcription of the 2005 Kenyon College
Commencement Address—May 21, 2005."
https://web.ics.purdue.edu/~drkelly/DFWKenyonAd-
dress2005.pdf.

"Western Maryland: A New State Initiative (@FreeWesternMary-
land)." Facebook page. *Facebook.* https://www.facebook.com/
FreeWesternMaryland/.

Chapter 2

"QuickFacts, Allegany County, Maryland." *United States Census
Bureau.* https://www.census.gov/quickfacts/alleganycounty-
maryland.

Chapter 3

Kennedy, John F. *Profiles in Courage.* New York: Harper Collins,
2006.

Chapter 4

"Census of Population and Housing, 1900." *U.S. Census Bureau.*
https://www.census.gov/prod/www/decennial.html.

Chapter 5

Hunt, James C. letter to the author's mother. February 1, 2006.

Miltenberger, Bernard W. "Preamble better welcome sign in Frostburg than 'liberal slogan.'" *Cumberland Times-News*. October 3, 2006. https://www.times-news.com/preamble-better-welcome-sign-in-frostburg-than-liberal-slogan/article_7135ee3a-88a5-550d-af43-346549fa3b07.html.

Sawyers, Michael A. "By 4-1 vote, Frostburg leaders defeat inclusive community concept." *Cumberland Times-News*. September 27, 2006. https://www.times-news.com/by-4-1-vote-frostburg-leaders-defeat-inclusive-community-concept/article_ad841d7d-5cd5-5813-92f1-e3bceadf56ca.html.

Chapter 6

Vance, J. D. *Hillbilly Elegy: A Memoir of a Family and Culture in Crisis*. New York: Harper Collins, 2016.

Chapter 8

Alstyne, Marshall Van and Brynjolfsson, Erik. "Global Village or Cyber-Balkans? Modeling and Measuring the Integration of Electronic Communities." *Management Science* 51, No. 6 (June 2005): 865-866. https://www-jstor-org.ezproxy.bowdoin.edu/stable/pdf/20110380.pdf?ab_segments=0%252Fbasic_SYC-5152%252Fcontrol&refreqid=excelsior%3A42379b3c-6ca22acob0a2e6a4dbe1259c.

"2015 White House Correspondents' Dinner." *C-SPAN.* 1:36:02. April 25, 2015. https://www.c-span.org/video/?325411-2/2015-white-house-correspondents-association-dinner.

Chapter 9

Krugman, Paul. "Coal Country Is a State of Mind." *The New York Times.* March 31, 2017. https://www.nytimes.com/2017/03/31/opinion/coal-country-is-a-state-of-mind.html.

LastWeekTonight. "Coal: Last Week Tonight with John Oliver (HBO)." *YouTube.* 24:20. June 17, 2017. https://www.youtube.com/watch?v=aw6RsUhw1Q8&t=204s.

Qui, Linda and John Schwartz. "Trump's False Claims About Coal, the Environment and West Virginia." *The New York Times.* August 21, 2018. https://www.nytimes.com/2018/08/21/us/politics/trump-fact-check-west-virginia-rally.html.

Thompson, Derek. "The White House Exaggerated the Growth of Coal Jobs by About 5,000 Percent." *The Atlantic.* June 6, 2017. https://www.theatlantic.com/business/archive/2017/06/pruitt-epa-coal-jobs-exaggerate/529311/.

Chapter 10

Hendriks, Galen, Seth Hanlon, and Michael Madowitz. "Trump's Corporate Tax Cut Is Not Trickling Down." *Center for American Progress.* September 26, 2019. https://www.americanprogress.org/issues/economy/news/2019/09/26/475083/trumps-corporate-tax-cut-not-trickling/.

ACKNOWLEDGMENTS

I've done a lot of crazy things in my life, but writing a book in a little less than a year tops the list. There were many moments when I questioned if this would ever be possible—and it truly would not have been without a community to whom I am so indebted.

First of all, thank you to Professor Eric Koester for getting the ball rolling and making this experience possible. Your enthusiasm and encouragement propelled me forward and assured me that I wasn't (too) crazy for taking on this challenge.

Thank you to my mom, Susan Keller (a.k.a. Susie-Q, Sue Keller, Qzer, Mama Keller), for being the most compassionate and understanding soul I have ever encountered. Thanks for entertaining my frustrations when I hit a bump in the road and sharing in my excitement when I cleared them. Thanks for being a badass and providing fodder for some of my stories. Thanks for literally forcing me to leave my desk to take a walk and clear my head when I sat plugging away for hours on end. And of course, thanks for providing the nutrition at home that allowed me to finish the later stages of this book.

Bowdoin's food may be nationally ranked, but it shall not be mentioned in the same breath. #OfficialChefOfOutliersTribe

Thank you to my sister, Georgia Grace (a.k.a. Geege, GG, Double G, G², Geegemeister, and much more), for infusing me with your life philosophy and teaching me to be spontaneous, remain adventurous, and seek out enriching experiences. You were supportive of this project from the very beginning, and I accredit you with giving me the impetus to begin the journey. You nurtured that initial ludicrous idea planted in my head as it grew into a tangible thing. From brainstorming ideas and reading early drafts to giving me advice on the cover, editing this thing from front to back, and writing the foreword, you have been instrumental in all stages of the process. I aspire to be like you.

P.S. I am still the favorite child.

Of course, I would be remiss if I did not mention the most important family member: our dog, Fela, whose persistent, [dog]matic belly rub demands provided much-needed respite from the writing process.

Thank you to my editors, Karina Agbisit and Linda Berardelli, for guiding me through this process and helping to shape the book into what it is today. You made it feel much more achievable.

Thank you to Jacob Rose for being a great friend and alpha reader. I greatly appreciate your candor, open-mindedness, and inquisitive nature. You have continually taken an interest in the book and pushed me to be better.

A big thank you to Alec Ross for sharing your generous time, keen insights, and kind words. You have been a source of inspiration for me in my book journey, and we are all fortunate to have you leading our world forward.

Thank you to Doug Schwab and Betsey-Hurwitz Schwab for equipping me with the camera to capture the shot that graces the cover. iPhone was just not going to do it, and you came in clutch!

Thank you to everyone who spread the word by mouth, shared a post on social media, or expressed a word of encouragement. Thank you to my friend Aura Carlson, who provided initial press in the Bowdoin Orient (a.k.a. the nation's oldest continuously published college weekly—there you go, Andrew Bastone). And thank you to anyone else I was not able to recognize.

Finally, my thanks to everyone who helped me turn this abstract idea of mine into a physical reality by pre-ordering a copy, donating to my crowdfunding campaign, and participating as a beta reader. This book came to fruition as a direct result of your support, and for that, I am eternally grateful.

John Crain
Nina Badger
Ree Miller
Natalie A Durney
Noa Schumann
Preston Anderson
Cameron Luzarraga
Ethan Edwards
Diana Edwards
Doug Schwab & Betsey-Hurwitz Schwab
Stephen Boe
Elaine Widner & Jim Kulstad
Jacob Rose
Grady Hayes
Daniel Blair

Francesca Moniz

Will Combs

Caroline Poole

Joanie Keller-Hand

Thomas Farr

Katherine (Cappie) Perras

Chance Crislip

Maddie Hikida

Hayden Weatherall

Isaac Katz

Roni Benzvi

Lucas Johnson

Mary Keller-Butler

Thomas Wentworth

Elise Hocking

Melissa Edwards

Rob Campbell

Jack Selig

Finn Bergquist

Gerry Crocker

Robert Agee

Darcy Fray

Gabriel Sylvan

Andrew Mangan

Garrett Mitman

Meg Jones

Robert (Bobby) Nishimwe

Lars Eklund

Will F Hausmann

Lydia Groves

Juliette Min

Jack Shane

Cameron Chertavian

Bryan Knapp

Nora Sullivan

Scott Kuhnle

Luke Tillitski

Thomas Daley

Jared Foxhall

Leif Maynard

Caroline Shipley

Noah Harris

Patrycja Pekala

William Busching

Connor Solimano

Candace Donoho

Jason Mumma

Deva Holliman

Siri Kazilionis

Sharon Diehl

Macauley & Carol Lord

Peter Pingitore

Richard Schlesinger

Lynn Schlesinger

Doug Kilmister

Susan Stewart

Chapman Odlum

Nicholas Bower

Andrew Bastone

Conor McManamy

Wilder Fray Short

Brian Folkins-Amador

Arin Custer

John G Cornmesser III

James Kirk
Ed Witkin & Ellen Schrader
Anna Cerf
Bryce Laskey
Adam Rossi
Justin Ko
Emilia Majersik
Reilly Butler
Eric Koester
Addison Bohn
Randi Mitchell
Amelia Witkin
Ely Osborne
Georgia Grace Edwards
Susan Keller

Made in the USA
Middletown, DE
11 July 2021

43965057R00086